ETHOLOGY AND DEVELOPMENT

Clinics in Developmental Medicine No. 47

Ethology and Development

Edited by
S. A. BARNETT

Preface by
LORD ZUCKERMAN

1973
Spastics International Medical Publications
LONDON: William Heinemann Medical Books Ltd.
PHILADELPHIA: J. B. Lippincott Co.

ISBN 0 433 0 251 8

Printed in England at THE LAVENHAM PRESS LTD., Lavenham, Suffolk

Contents

Preface

The authors of the essays which make up *Ethology and Development* have approached their tasks not only with admirable modesty, but also with a sound critical sense of the relevance of the facts which they have assembled, mostly on the basis of animal experiment, to problems of human development. Their work has confirmed that the human nervous system is very plastic, that the ability to learn can be demonstrated almost from birth, and that the human infant is the master of some kind of conceptual process even before verbalisation starts. They have also been wary of generalising too far, and all are critical of the extent to which analogical reasoning from animals assists in the understanding of human behavior.

This is all to the good. The subject of ethology has suffered some rude knocks in recent years at the hands of more popular writers who have been successful in conveying not a scientific but a sensational and facile picture of human behavior. They have encouraged the general reading public to believe that man is some kind of naked ape, obsessed with sex, or a monster unrepentantly acquisitive and aggressive, or a vertebrate whose complex behavior can be understood if we study the robin, the goose, or the baboon. Their message is seductive and simple, and it is not at all surprising that the books they write are best sellers on the bookstalls of railway stations or airports. What is not understood is that much of what they write represents a corruption of scientific knowledge and scientific method.

Ethology and Development is thus not only to be welcomed because of its substance. It is equally a timely reminder that animal behaviour can be studied as a scientific discipline, and that, when approached with objectivity and caution, it can turn up facts as interesting to the serious reader as are the ethological romances of the popularisers.

Lord Zuckerman

ACKNOWLEDGEMENTS

Thanks are due as follows for permission to reproduce certain material in this book.

Chapter 1. To the publishers of 'Behaviour' for Figure 2.

To Professor K. Immelmann and to the publishers of 'Zeitschrift für Tierpsychologie for Figure 8.

Chapter 2. To the publishers of 'Biologia Neonatorum' for Figure 2.

To S. Fraňkovà and to the publishers of 'Activas Nervosa Superior (Praha)' for Figure 3.

To the publishers of 'Brain Research' for Figure 4.

Chapter 3. To H. Weiner and to the publishers of 'Psychosomatic Medicine' for Figure 2.

To the publishers of 'Psychosomatic Medicine' for Figures 3, 4, 5, 7, 8, 9 and 10.

To Academic Press Ltd. for Figure 6.

Chapter 5. To Sol Mednick and to the publishers of 'Scientific Medicine' for Figures 1 and 2.

To David Linton and to the publishers of 'Scientific Medicine' for Figure 3.

Contributors

ROBERT ADER — Department of Psychiatry,
University of Rochester School of Medicine and
Dentistry, Rochester, New York 14642, U.S.A.

S. A. BARNETT — Department of Zoology,
The Australian National University,
Box 4 P.O. Canberra A.C.T. 2600,
Australia

P. P. G. BATESON — Sub-department of Animal Behaviour,
Madingley, Cambridge CB3 8AA, England

J. F. BERNAL — Unit for Research on Medical Applications of
Psychology,
Station Road, Cambridge, England

JOHN DOBBING — Department of Child Health,
University of Manchester,
Clinical Sciences Building,
York Place, Manchester M13 0JJ, England

M. P. M. RICHARDS — Unit for Research on Medical Applications of
Psychology,
Station Road, Cambridge, England

GERALD C. RUPPENTHAL — Regional Primate Research Center,
University of Washington,
Seattle, Washington 98105, U.S.A.

GENE P. SACKETT — Regional Primate Research Center,
University of Washington,
Seattle, Washington 98105, U.S.A.

J. L. SMART — Department of Child Health,
University of Manchester,
Clinical Sciences Building,
York Place, Manchester M13 0JJ, England

lying mechanisms are different is undecided. While the connotations of the classical concept of imprinting are in many ways misleading, study of the process has raised important issues about predisposition to learn during the development of human behavior.

REFERENCES

Bateson, P. P. G. (1966) 'The characteristics and context of imprinting.' *Biological Reviews*, **41**, 177.

—— (1971) 'Imprinting.' *in* Moltz, H. (Ed.) *Ontogeny of Vertebrate Behavior*. New York: Academic Press, p. 369.

—— (1972) 'The formation of social attachments in young birds.' *in Proceedings of the International Ornithological Conference*, 1970, p. 303.

—— (1973) 'Internal influences on early learning in birds.' *in* Hinde, R. A., Hinde, J. S. (Eds.) *Constraints on Learning*. London: Academic Press. (*In the press*.)

—— Wainwright, A. A. P. (1972) 'The effects of prior exposure to light on the imprinting process in domestic chicks.' *Behaviour*, **42**, 279.

Hoffman, H. S., Searle, J., Toffey, S., Kozma, F. (1966) 'Behavioral control by an imprinted stimulus.' *Journal of the Experimental Analysis of Behavior*, **9**, 177.

Immelmann, K. (1969) 'Über den Einfluss frühkindlicher Erfahrungen auf die geschlechtliche Objektfixierung bei Estrilden.' *Zeitschrift für Tierpsychologie*, **26**, 677.

Lorenz, K. (1935) 'Der Kumpan in der Umwelt des Vogels.' Journal für Ornithologie, **83**, 10–213 and 289–413.

—— (1970) translation of above in *Studies in Animal and Human Behaviour, Vol 1*. London: Methuen.

Sluckin, W. (1972) *Imprinting and Early Learning*. 2nd edn. London: Methuen.

Smith, F. V. (1969) *Attachment of the Young*. Edinburgh: Oliver & Boyd.

CHAPTER 2

Early Undernutrition, Brain Development and Behavior

JOHN DOBBING and J. L. SMART

In this paper we consider whether undernutrition during certain stages of brain development can contribute to lasting behavioral changes. For those primarily interested in the human implications, enquiry has largely centred on severely malnourished babies in grossly underprivileged communities, usually in developing countries; it has also impinged on the general paediatric concern for the fate of low-birth-weight babies, especially those of retarded intra-uterine growth (the 'small-for-dates' baby), and any others whose growth may be impaired, including those with metabolic errors, congenital anomalies, endocrine disturbances, chronic hypoxia, long-term exposure to growth-retarding drugs, or any syndrome which includes growth retardation in its consequences.

The question being asked is deceptively simple for the unwary, and many are dismayed at the readiness with which it is sometimes over-dramatised. The question whether early *malnutrition* causes *mental subnormality* or *mental retardation* or *brain damage* is, in our view, wrongly posed. Rather, it should be asked whether undernutrition or growth retardation, among the multitude of other important early environmental factors, can be identified as a contributor to the algebraic sum of those influences which determine adult 'attainment'. Efforts to answer this more realistic, but much more difficult question must attempt to isolate the variable of nutrition experimentally, and even this, of course, is strictly impossible.

We shall first examine the proposition that there are periods of heightened vulnerability in the physical development of the brain, during which growth retardation results in long-lasting distortions and deficits in adult brain structure. This will necessarily be established in animal species before an attempt is made to extrapolate the idea to our own. Some evidence for the validity of such extrapolation will be discussed. The search for altered animal behavior which may or may not be associated with the structural changes will then be described. The possible meaning of such alterations, and whether they may be supposed to have any relevance to the human condition, will be discussed.

'Vulnerable Period' Pathology

Developmental neuropathology has hitherto been exclusively concerned with focal lesions, structural or biochemical. The former are either first-trimester teratological malformations or areas of last-trimester focal destruction caused by such agencies as hypoxia, hypoglycaemia, hyperbilirubinaemia, focal haemorrhage or trauma. Biochemical 'lesions' are, by contrast, diffuse and either identifiable histochemically (the lipidoses) or not (the inborn errors).

The new pathology proposed here shows none of these features, and often does not even show related physical signs. It consists of quantitative disorders of the brain's growth programme, which, although they result in easily detectable differences in adult brain structure, would not be revealed by orthodox neuropathology. Neither the very rare nutritional condition of Wernicke's encephalopathy nor such lesions as those of vitamin A deficiency form part of the new pathology, though some forms of microcephaly (for example, in rubella) may be allied with it. An important possibility (though it is no more than that) is that some cases of hitherto unclassified mental retardation may show such quantitative rather than 'lesion' pathology.

The science of developmental nutrition recognises three important interrelated parameters of undernutrition. These are its severity, its duration and its timing. The importance of the third factor (the age at which undernutrition occurs) has given rise to the idea of transient periods of heightened sensitivity, which have some apparent resemblance to sensitive periods during the development of behavior. Largely because of the need to imply both lasting distortion and lasting deficit, the term 'vulnerable' has been used to describe this period, rather than the more academic terms 'critical' or 'sensitive'.

The basis of the vulnerable period hypothesis (Dobbing 1968a) may be illustrated by a clear-cut finding in rats that, if *body* growth is retarded at the time of the *brain* growth-spurt, there is a resulting growth deficit which resists subsequent nutritional rehabilitation. There are permanent deficits of both brain and body growth attainment, and, in the brain at least there is some permanent structural distortion as well as deficit. This principle is probably valid for other species, including man.

There is an apparent dependence of good body growth on the achievement of a satisfactory brain growth-spurt. The *body* growth-spurt of all species is later than that of the brain, and it is not itself 'vulnerable' in the above, lasting sense. Nutritional retardation of body growth at this later stage can be fully made up on restoration of a good diet (Widdowson and McCance 1963), and even severe starvation in the adult produces no detectable lasting effects on the brain (Dobbing 1968b). Whether growth retardation before the brain growth-spurt has lasting structural effects is less clear, although none large enough to be shown by gross measurement have been detected in the brain, at least when growth has been retarded to the extent commonly occurring in human beings.

In the form originally proposed, the period of vulnerability was considered to be the whole period of the brain growth-spurt to be described below.

A second and overlapping hypothesis (Winick and Noble 1966) can also be applied to all other tissues. It was discovered that during their post-organogenetic growth all tissues pass through a period of cell division, followed by one of growth in cell size. Undernutrition during the former phase, but not during the latter, permanently reduces growth-attainment in all tissues.

17

There can be no question that this latter is a basic law for catch-up potential throughout the body, but it may be unsatisfactory when applied to those aspects of brain development which are likely to be functionally important. A greater complexity arises from the heterogeneity of brain tissue. For example, glial mitosis occurs later than neuronal mitosis, and glia eventually outnumber neurons heavily. Most experimental proof of the vulnerability of 'brain cell' mitosis has been confined to the later phase of glial multiplication, which happens to occupy the first part of the brain growth-spurt. Therefore, most of the lasting 'brain cell' deficit in these experiments must be glial, and it seems unlikely that a numerical glial deficit would be functionally important. It is even possible that a numerical neuronal cell deficit might not be very significant for brain function, compared with a deficit (for example) in subsequent dendritic branching and in the establishment of synaptic connections. The latter are probably more important features of neuronal growth and are not mitotic events. They are the brain's equivalent to growth in cell size, and it is possible that such post-mitotic events within the brain growth-spurt are also vulnerable. Finally, the technique of expressing average cell size as a protein:DNA ratio must surely be less meaningful for neurons, with their enormously long cytoplasmic extensions, than for a homogeneous mass of liver cells.

The term 'growth-spurt' is derived from the sigmoid trajectory of most organ or whole body growth. The spurt is simply the transient period of high growth velocity. In the brain of all mammalian species examined, it represents a similar phase of brain development. Species do, however, vary in the stage at which birth occurs (Fig. 1); thus, in the rat the growth-spurt is a postnatal event (Dobbing and Sands 1972*a*), in the guinea pig it is prenatal (Dobbing and Sands 1970*a*), and in pigs (Dickerson and Dobbing 1967) and people (Dobbing 1970) it is both pre- and post-natal. Normal birth has no significance for most growth programmes, including that of the brain. Thus there are obvious pitfalls here for those wishing to use animals to investigate 'fetal' or 'postnatal' brain growth, unless the species is carefully chosen and the timing of the brain growth-spurt in that species known.

The brain growth-spurt begins at about the time neuroblast multiplication ends, and the adult number of neurons has already been almost achieved. This is towards the end of the second human (fetal) trimester (Dobbing and Sands 1970*b*), and in the first postnatal days of the rat. It ends with the end of the major period of rapid myelination, at about two years of human postnatal age (Dobbing and Sands 1972*b*), and about twenty-five days in the rat (Dobbing and Sands 1972*a*). The velocity curve of increments in brain wet weight encompasses the whole period, except perhaps for the later stages of myelination. The major easily detectable events, apart from an increase in size, are an almost explosive multiplication of oligodendroglial cells (Benstead *et al.* 1957) followed by a period of intense lipid synthesis related to myelination (Davison and Peters 1970). There are large and sometimes sudden changes of enzyme activity (Adlard and Dobbing 1971*a* and *b*). There is a fall of tissue water reciprocally with the rise in brain lipid (Dobbing and Sands 1972*a*). Sodium and potassium move rapidly

18

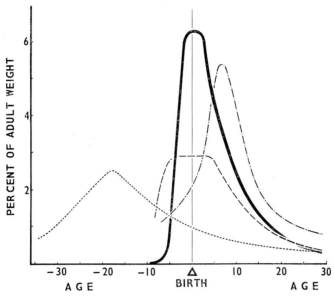

Fig. 1. Velocity curves of brain growth (wet weight) in different species. Prenatal and postnatal age expressed as follows: human ———— in months (Dobbing & Sands 1972*b*); guinea pig - - - - - - - - - in days (Dobbing and Sands 1970*a*); pig – – – – – – – in weeks (Dickerson and Dobbing 1967); rat –·–·–·–·–·– in days (Dobbing and Sands 1972*a*).

towards their adult values (de Souza and Dobbing 1971). Perhaps more important, but less easily measured, the growth-spurt includes the growth and branching of dendritic processes and the establishment of inter-neuronal connections. These are held to be to some extent plastic in the adult, and it would be surprising if they were not even more so during development.

It would be facile to assume functional significance for the vulnerability of the growth-spurt complex as described above. There are two major difficulties.

(i) Neurobiologists have only measured parameters which are comparatively easy to measure. No-one knows what to measure as a physical index of important aspects of higher mental function. Certainly cell number, brain size, degree of myelination and so forth are no more than tangible examples of structural characteristics, which, by analogy, may react in a similar manner to whatever structures actually do matter.

(ii) Developmental processes in the brain occur at different times in different regions and at different rates. There is a highly organised temporal and spatial developmental sequence, and probably a differential regional vulnerability related to the normal rate and timing in any particular region. One clear example is provided by the cerebellum, which grows more rapidly than other parts and is more affected by growth retardation (Dickerson and Dobbing 1966). Some of its neurons divide later than most (Altman 1970), and these are, therefore, differentially selected by later growth-retardation (Dobbing *et al.* 1971).

19

Some Lasting Effects of Early Growth Retardation

Provided the brain growth-spurt period is carefully selected, it is necessary only to retard body growth rates towards the lower limits of the 'normal' range to produce permanent changes. No nutritional disease or obvious ill-health is required. Changes have been found in the brains of adult rats whose only nutritional handicap has been to be suckled in larger-than-normal families during the brain growth-spurt. They are fed a highly nutritious diet *ad libitum* from weaning at three weeks of age until they reach maturity. When looked for in previously underfed adults, the permanent residual physical effects of such mild growth retardation represent both deficits of and distortions from the normal, and include the following.

(a) *Small brain size.* This is a true microcephaly, the brain being permanently smaller than is appropriate for the *body weight*, in spite of having shown the traditional characteristics of 'brain sparing' during the growth period (Dobbing and Sands 1972*a*). Also the brain is not uniformly small, being more so in the cerebellum than in the rest of the brain. Thus the small brain is distorted, rather than merely deficient.

(b) *Fewer cells.* When measured by DNA analysis, these smaller brains have fewer cells (Dobbing and Sands 1972*a*). There are disproportionately fewer in the cerebellum, and among the cerebellar neurons the later dividing granular neurons are disproportionately reduced. There are also indications that some cerebral neurons are likewise disproportionately reduced (Dobbing *et al.* 1971). However, most of the total cell deficit is probably glial. Here again, there is distortion of brain structure, in addition to simple deficiency.

(c) *Less lipid.* Many of the brain lipids are permanently reduced to a greater extent than would be predicted from the smaller brain size. Such deficiences per unit fresh weight are selectively found in those lipids most characteristic of myelin (*see* Dobbing 1968*b*). This is a further example of distortion.

(d) *Altered enzyme activity.* Assessments of enzyme activities are bedevilled by argument about their significance and the significance of the various ways of expressing them. Should activity be expressed per cell (DNA), per unit protein, per unit fresh weight, per brain region, or how? The difficulties are greatly magnified in a tissue whose architecture and cell types are as heterogeneous as are those of the brain, compared, for example, with the more homogeneous liver. Such differences as have been found in the present context probably represent structural changes. For example, the activity of acetylcholinesterase per unit fresh weight in previously undernourished adult rats is much *higher* than in controls (Adlard and Dobbing 1971*c*), in spite of having been lower during the early period of restriction (Adlard and Dobbing 1971*a*). It seems very likely that the enzyme is related to structures (perhaps cholinergic nerve endings), whose *concentration* has been increased as a result of a differentially greater deficit of other structures. Interpretation can be extremely tortuous, but at least here is another distortion.

In summary, the evidence for the vulnerability of the brain during its growth-spurt is good. Certainly, however, it need not be the only vulnerable period of brain growth, even in the present restricted sense. A much more careful analysis of the vulnerability of other stages, especially the earlier and quantitatively smaller phase of neuronal multiplication (corresponding with the human second trimester) may reveal other periods of vulnerability. Nevertheless the hypothesis remains a useful one, and in general terms is well supported by the evidence.

Brain Growth Opportunity

It has recently been shown that the brain growth-spurt is obliged to occur at a predetermined chronological age, even when conditions are unfavourable and growth has been nutritionally retarded (Dobbing and Sands 1972a). The effect of such 'retardation' is to *reduce the extent* of brain growth processes, not to delay their *occurrence*. This has been demonstrated by constructing velocity curves of the accumulation of fresh weight, DNA, and cholesterol (a major brain lipid) in undernourished animals and normal controls. The smaller area under the velocity curves of the undernourished animals, together with their failure to exhibit 'catch-up' on restoration to a normal diet, accounts for the ultimate deficit. An example of this is illustrated in Figure 2 for the phase of (glial) cell division.

This introduces a principle of possibly great practical importance to human babies. If there is a once-only opportunity to grow the brain properly, it is

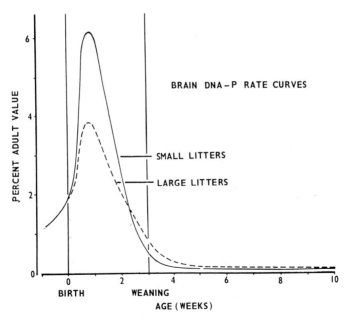

Fig. 2. Velocity curves of DNA increment in the brains of rats suckled in small and large litters during the brain growth-spurt. Growth retardation has not delayed the timing of the peak velocity (Dobbing and Sands 1972a).

21

presumably important that the best conditions should be provided at this time. There may even be something to be said for directing nutritional aid towards the relevant age-group in times of severe shortage, at the expense of older individuals whose brain growth-spurt is over.

The Extrapolation of the Vulnerable Period Hypothesis to Man

It has been shown that the changes described in previously growth-retarded adult animals are related to the coincidence of the restriction with the period of the brain growth-rate spurt. Leaving aside any consideration of whether such changes matter, it ought to be possible to predict which human babies are at risk in this sense. All that is required is to identify the human brain growth-spurt. A study of nearly 200 complete human brains reveals the following.

(a) Human neuronal multiplication occurs mainly in the second trimester of gestation (Dobbing and Sands 1970*b*). The subsequent growth of dendrites, and the establishment of synaptic connections, is, by inference, later. Probably, it occupies the remainder of the growth-spurt.

(b) Hence the period corresponding to the vulnerable one discussed above in animals begins with the third trimester.

(c) The end of the (glial) cell multiplication phase is at about eighteen postnatal months (Dobbing 1970), and the whole growth-spurt may be virtually over by two postnatal years (Dobbing and Sands 1972*b*).

Hence for full-term human babies only about one eighth of the vulnerable period is fetal, a situation much closer to that of the infant rat than has hitherto been recognised. What, then, is likely to be the long-term prognosis of small-for-dates babies born near to term? According to any reasonable extrapolation from the animal work, it should require a further year to eighteen months of growth restriction to produce distortions and deficits of the brain comparable with those produced experimentally in animals. Much will therefore depend on the growth rate during the remaining seven-eighths or so of the human brain growth-spurt, that is, the first postnatal eighteen months. Thus the first one and a half years of postnatal life becomes a period not of vulnerability but of opportunity. There is some evidence from experimental animal undernutrition that, if rehabilitation is instituted well before the end of the brain growth-spurt, there is apparent recovery (Winick *et al.* 1968). However, recovery here was measured in terms of whole brain amounts, and it is not yet clear whether there are persisting regional deficits. It could be that restriction on early growth processes in those regions of the brain which develop early may produce lasting regional deficits, which would be masked by analysis of whole brain.

It is, therefore, likely that any baby whose lean-body-mass growth is seriously retarded for the whole, or for a substantial proportion, of the period from thirty weeks gestation to two full years of postnatal age will emerge with changes in the physical state of its brain comparable to those in rats outlined above. Whether these will matter is an entirely open question, since it is completely unknown which parts of the physical brain are related to 'higher mental function'. It is also not known how much compensation is available in the multiplicity of other developmental, environmental factors bearing upon the ultimate outcome. The most that can be suggested in practical management terms is that, amongst all the other steps taken to promote baby welfare, the best true growth of babies should be ensured at this particular period. This applies equally to the baby in an underprivileged, developing community, the prematurely born, the 'small-for-dates', and the normal full-term baby.

Behavioral Implications

The lasting effects of early undernutrition on the structure of the brain have necessarily been investigated in laboratory animals. The question may now be asked whether there are any behavioral consequences in these animals whose brains have been permanently altered. Can the animal model be used to help answer the all-important question of whether humans suffer any lasting intellectual deficit after early growth retardation? There are likely to be some formidable difficulties in extrapolating from one species' behavior to another, even though their patterns of physical brain growth are so similar. However, we believe that the human problem, entangled as it is with a multitude of socio-economic and other distinctively human factors, can still be elucidated through animal studies in simple laboratory situations, granted that, even in the laboratory, there may be unwanted and virtually uncontrollable effects of the nutritional procedures we must use.

Experimental studies of nutritional deprivation early in life have most often been on rats. It has been convenient that the brain growth-spurt in this species is largely confined to the suckling period. One of four nutritional procedures has usually been employed. (i) Maternal undernutrition is achieved by feeding the mother a restricted quantity of a good quality food daily. (ii) In the case of malnutrition, the female has access to an unlimited supply of an unbalanced diet, often low in protein, and consequently high in some other constituent, usually carbohydrate. (iii) Regular separation of mother and young ensures that suckling time is curtailed. These three techniques usually include standardisation of litter size at birth. (iv) The large litter method requires that two or more mothers give birth within a short space of time. Young are removed from their mothers and randomly assigned to an abnormally large or small litter. In this way, mother rats or mice are given large litters of between fifteen and twenty young.

The method used is partly determined by the time at which nutritional restriction is required. Obviously, procedures (iii) and (iv) apply only to the suckling period, whereas dietary restrictions of the putative mother can begin even before she has conceived.

All these deprivation methods probably alter the environment of the suckling animal from normal. Fraňková (1971), for example, observed the behavior of mother rats fed either a normal or a low protein diet in a situation in which the young had been displaced from the nest to various parts of the cage. Adequately fed mothers retrieved their nestlings more efficiently, and devoted more attention to them during the test period, than malnourished mothers

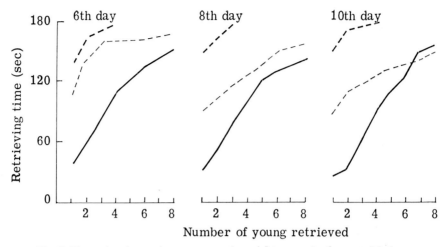

Fig. 3. Time taken by mother rats to retrieve eight young to the nest. Mothers were fed one of the following three diets: good quality ———— (n = 12); low protein/high carbohydrate – – – (n = 13); or low protein/high fat – – – (n = 13). (*Redrawn from* Fraňková 1971.)

(Fig. 3). If the differences in maternal behavior in the test situation may be taken as an index of deficient maternal care, in general, by the malnourished mothers, then there is cause for concern about the non-alimentary effects of the deprivation procedure on the young. The similar, apparently beneficial, effects on the development of rats and mice of a wide variety of stimulation procedures in infancy has long been a puzzle. One hypothesis is that the important common factor is an increase in maternal attention towards the 'treated' offspring (Barnett and Burn 1967). Presumably, the effects of diminished maternal care would be in the opposite direction. Short of rearing without a mother, it is impossible to envisage a technique for nutritional deprivation in the suckling period which could not alter some aspect of mother-infant interaction.

The prospect is not, however, unduly daunting, as areas of agreement do exist among experimental findings derived through different nutritional procedures in the suckling period. In these instances, the causal factor is likely to be nutritional deprivation, the feature obviously common to all, or some consequence of the deprivation so closely linked to it as to be well nigh inevitable. Moreover, the occurrence of similar unavoidable side-effects is almost certainly a feature of the human situation as well.

Development of Behavior
There is little doubt that the offspring of female animals which have been subjected to prolonged nutritional deprivation are retarded in both growth and development. For example, pups born to bitches malnourished from weaning exhibit persistent infantile 'waddling' gait (Platt and Stewart 1968), and the young of mother rats fed about half of what they would normally have eaten during pregnancy and lactation are late in developing a number of

24

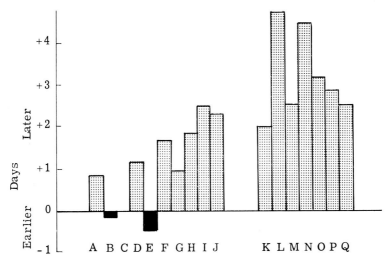

Fig. 4. Differences between young rats fostered at birth to normal or underfed mothers: A to J* refer to age at maturation of physical features and reflexes; K to Q* refer to age at which certain responses were first seen in an open field. Values for well-fed young are taken as the base line (0) and those for undernourished offspring are expressed as deviations from it. (*Redrawn from* Smart and Dobbing 1971*b*).

reflexes and simple behavior patterns (Simonson *et al.* 1969, Smart and Dobbing 1971*a*). Even mild malnutrition (14 per cent compared with 21 per cent protein) imposed on rats for two generations causes maturational delays (Cowley and Griesel 1963). Nestlings whose parents *and* grandparents had been fed the low protein diet developed more slowly than controls.

Whether these delays are the result of deficient nutrition *in utero* or in the suckling period, or of both, can be answered only by cross-fostering young at birth between normal and inadequately fed females. It is not sufficient to give nutritionally deprived mothers free access to a good quality diet after parturition, as the earlier period of restriction almost certainly reduces milk production. Reflex ontogeny is unaffected in the fostered offspring of malnourished (Zeman 1967) or undernourished mother rats (Smart and Dobbing 1971*b*), though there is evidence of delay in the appearance of exploratory responses in the latter study. Simonson *et al.* (1969) likewise report retarded development of the exploratory behavior of rats as a result of underfeeding the pregnant mothers.

Neurological maturation in the rat is evidently much more vulnerable to nutritional insult in the suckling period than before birth. Reflex ontogeny is slowed in young reared by underfed foster-mothers (Smart and Dobbing 1971*b*), and the appearance of exploratory responses is delayed (Fig. 4). Offspring of

*The developmental indices were: A, righting; B, ear unfolding; C, negative geotaxis; D, cliff avoidance; E, incisor eruption; F, auditory startle; G, vibrissa placing; H, eye opening; I, free-fall righting; J, visual placing; K, head-lifting; L, left area 1; M, half-rearing; N, thigmotaxis; O, left the central area; P, reached periphery; Q, rearing.

25

mothers fed a low protein diet from parturition show similar deficits in exploratory behavior (Fraňková and Barnes 1968a). Altman et al. (1971) observed the motor ability, in a variety of situations, of young rats from mothers fed 40 per cent or 20 per cent of normal during lactation. Whereas the moderately undernourished group differed little from well-fed controls, the severely restricted group were less proficient than the controls on most tasks: they took longer to turn round on and descend a vertical rope, when they were able to do so at all, and regained their home cage less promptly from an adjoining test chamber. The severely restricted group attained a control level of performance only after a delay of several days.

Such findings may have some bearing on the interpretation of results from experiments in which behavior is tested beyond the suckling period, but still within, or shortly after, a period of nutritional deprivation. For example, Baird et al. (1971) studied maze-learning by rats aged seventy-five days, which had been inadequately fed from birth, and Smart and Dobbing (1972) tested the passive avoidance behavior of young rats only nine days after weaning from underfed foster-mothers. In such cases, there may be a developmental component of any differences in behavior between control and experimental animals; that is, deficiencies may reflect a lag in development and not necessarily any permanent defect. This stricture applies to nearly all studies of the behavioral consequences of early growth restriction in man. Because of man's enormously protracted period of development, follow-up studies to maturity are extremely rare.

A baby of low birth-weight may have been born prematurely, or its growth may have been retarded in utero. In the latter instance, it is said to be 'small-for-dates'. To ensure appropriate treatment, it is important to know which has been the case. Hence, the accurate assessment of a baby's gestational age is crucial. Accordingly, clinical paediatrics has been concerned more with finding indices of neurological maturation which are relatively independent of growth in utero and are hence reliable indicators of age (Brett 1965, Robinson 1966), than with seeking effects of fetal growth restriction. Recently, however, Michaelis et al. (1970) made a detailed investigation of several reflexes and motor patterns of full-term small-for-dates and normal babies. 'Good' or 'marked' responses were much more typical of the normal infants. This is just as would have been predicted from the rat studies, in view of the fact (discussed above) that human neonates are more mature in terms of brain growth than newborn rats.

The occurrence of developmental delays may be important in two ways. (i) The slowly developing child may be at a disadvantage both socially and educationally. Education tends regrettably to be tied more to age than to stage of development; hence the school environment of the dysmature child may be inappropriate to his needs. (ii) Quite apart from these possibly injurious effects of slowed maturation per se, the delays may reflect a more basic deficiency whose outcome is some permanent alteration in behavior. Hence nutritionally-induced developmental delays may foreshadow long-lasting behavioral changes.

Long-lasting Effects on Behavior

In all the experiments to be discussed in this section, the animals were subjected to a period of nutritional deprivation early in life and then allowed free access to a good quality diet till they were observed as adults. The period of nutritional rehabilitation usually exceeded that of restriction. The first part of the discussion deals with aspects of behavior which have been consistently affected by early nutritional experience and considers the evidence for an effect on 'learning ability', and the second part attempts to relate the magnitude of effect to characteristics of the nutritional deprivation.

(a) *Aspects of Behavior Affected*

(i) *Activity*. When an animal is placed in a strange environment, it may remain still for a while, but eventually it begins to move about. This tendency to explore novel surroundings has often been tested by observing animals for fifteen minutes or less in what is misleadingly called an 'open field'. Far from being open, such fields are almost aways bounded by a wall. The floor is divided into a number of smaller areas, and may be bare or furnished with barriers, hurdles or toys. In several investigations, control rodents moved about the open field more than animals which had experienced early nutritional deprivation; they also reared up on their hind legs more frequently (for example, Fraňková and Barnes 1968a). In no experiment were they ever outscored on these measures of exploratory behavior.

Only one study provides any information on the time-course of these differences. Adult offspring of mother rats which were underfed during pregnancy were consistently slower to leave a 'start' box than normal animals, and subsequently moved about less in an open field (Simonson et al. 1971). This situation bears some elements of similarity to 'cage emergence' tests, in so far as the animals' tendency to leave an enclosed space for a comparatively open one is measured. Seitz (1954) found that rats which had been reared in litters of twelve were both more reluctant to emerge from their home cages and, in a separate test, less active in an open field than rats from litters of six.

In general, early nutritional deprivation evidently reduces activity over short periods in novel surroundings. Yet, the few investigations of activity over longer periods indicate changes in the opposite direction. Rats weaned from malnourished mothers, and themselves fed a low protein diet for up to six weeks thereafter, make many more revolutions in 'running' wheels than controls during two one-hour sessions (Guthrie 1968). Activity in a running wheel is of a special kind and difficult to relate to any other measure of activity. But the same cannot be said for that recorded by Barnett et al. (1971) in 'plus-mazes'. Each maze had a central nest box with four arms radiating from it. Food was available at the end of one arm and balsa wood for gnawing at the end of another. Excursions into the arms and time spent there were recorded automatically. Groups of rats which had been either malnourished for eight weeks from four weeks of age, or underfed for the same period, both behaved differently from controls. During their twelve-day spell in the maze, 'low protein' rats consistently made most visits to the arms, whereas the undernourished rats spent most time in them. Both experimental groups were more active than the controls, though in contrasted ways.

Supposing that the last effect is one of some generality, can it be reconciled with the decrement in activity in novel surroundings? Perhaps the previously deprived animals are initially more inhibited in a strange environment, but soon become used to it and recover their usual, abnormally high level of activity. Alternatively, both groups may respond to novelty with an increase in activity, but the initial level of normal animals is higher and falls more steeply. If so, opposite effects would be recorded from tests of different duration. But these suggestions are descriptive, and leave unanswered the important question of what underlies such differences in behavior. Some speculations are put forward by Barnett *et al.* (1971).

(ii) *Behavior with Respect to Food.* It is not unreasonable to suggest that if an animal experiences a period of food shortage it will for some time afterwards behave differently towards food. This hypothesis, tacked on to the Freudian notion that the deprivation period must be early in life for maximum effect, has been the subject of several investigations (reviewed by Bronfenbrenner 1968). Typical of these was the study by Hunt (1941) of 'the effects of infant feeding-frustration. .in the albino rat'. He gave rats limited access to food at irregular intervals for fifteen days, starting at twenty-four or thirty-two days of age. Thereafter, they had free access to food for five months. Their tendency to hoard pellets of food was then tested, both before and after a five-day period of irregular feeding opportunities. It is well known that rodents will make repeated journeys to carry pieces of food from a source to their nest. When sated, the experimental rats did not differ from controls, but when hungry the animals with early experience of restricted feeding, especially the twenty-four day group, hoarded more pellets. They also tended to eat faster.

In this and other early studies, the period of food restriction was always after weaning. Recently, Smart (1971) compared food-getting by the adult offspring of mother rats underfed either during pregnancy and lactation, or during only one of these periods. All rats were hungry at the time of testing. They were trained to press a lever to gain a food reward, and then tested in a situation in which the frequency of reward was largely independent of the rate of lever pressing. The offspring of mothers deprived during both periods or in pregnancy alone pressed the lever more frequently than controls; that is, for about the same amount of reward, they established higher rates of responding (Fig. 5).

Evidently, hungry adult animals, which have experienced a period of food deprivation early in life, show an exaggerated response to food. Moreover, the timing of the effective early experience in Smart's experiments indicates that the change is more basic than just the memory of the deprivation. However, there is evidence of lasting metabolic differences between normal and early underfed animals, which may relate to their behavior towards food. Food utilization, notably protein metabolism, is less efficient in offspring of mother

28

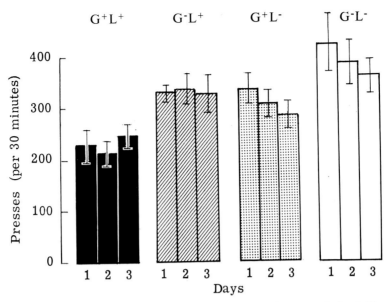

Fig. 5. Frequency with which hungry adult rats press a lever to gain food. The rats had the opportunity to gain a pellet of food only, on average, every two minutes. Rats were either adequately nourished throughout (G^+L^+), born to an underfed mother and fostered to a well fed mother (G^-L^+), born to a well fed mother and fostered to an underfed mother (G^+L^-), or undernourished both pre- and postnatally (G^-L^-). From weaning, all rats had free access to a good quality diet.

rats underfed throughout pregnancy and lactation (Lee and Chow 1965). Eleven-year-old Formosan children from poorly fed families are apparently similarly affected (Chow *et al.* 1968). Though efforts are made to have both the control and experimental *adult* rats in an equivalent state of food deficit for their behavior tests, by fasting them for the same length of time, or to the same proportion of their fully-fed weight, it seems that these measures may not be entirely adequate.

(iii) *Response to Stressful Stimulation.* The difference in food-orientated behavior by hungry animals may owe something to the stressful properties of the adult fasting procedures, rather than their strictly nutritional ones. In so far as fasted rats have high concentrations of corticosteroids in their blood (Boulouard 1963), the procedures certainly are stressful. Barnes *et al.* (1968) studied behavior towards food by adult rats which had been reared by malnourished mothers and either underfed or malnourished for four weeks after weaning. When feeding was restricted to one hour a day, the early-deprived animals, especially those weaned on to a low protein diet, spilled much more food than controls. There were no differences in amount spilled when feeding was *ad libitum.* The authors suggest that the stressful nature of the one-hour feeding schedule is important, and that the increased spillage was a consequence of 'an elevated state of excitement'.

29

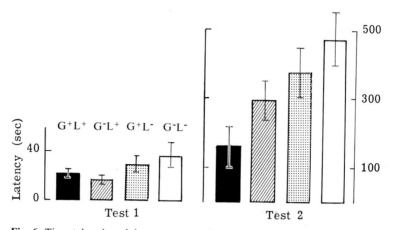

Fig. 6. Time taken by adult rats to cross from one side of a two-compartment box to the other, in test 1 when they received a brief electric shock for doing so, and in test 2 one day later. Rats were either adequately nourished throughout (G^+L^+), born to an underfed mother and fostered to a well fed mother (G^-L^+), born to a well fed mother and fostered to an underfed mother (G^+L^-), or undernourished both pre- and postnatally (G^-L^-). From weaning, all rats had free access to a good quality diet.

Levitsky and Barnes (1970) tested this hypothesis by investigating the effects of other stressors on the behavior of previously malnourished rats. Such animals, exposed to a loud bang, reduced their movements about an open field more than controls. They were also more reluctant to step down from a platform after receiving an electric shock for so doing one minute previously, and, in a third test, pressed a lever at a higher rate to postpone an electric shock. Smart (1971) found similarly that rats with a history of early nutritional deprivation were abnormally inhibited in a passive avoidance situation. Each animal received a brief shock when it moved from one compartment to the other of a two-compartment box. When re-tested a day later, the early-deprived rats showed a stronger tendency to remain on the 'safe' side (Fig. 6). Pigs malnourished early in life are also said to show signs of 'heightened excitement' in unpleasant circumstances (Barnes *et al.* 1970).

One way of describing all these findings is to say that the previously poorly-fed animals over-react in stressful situations. The hypothalamus-pituitary-adrenal system may be supposed to be especially active in such conditions. Perhaps it is vulnerable to the early nutritional insult. Prompted by these considerations, Adlard and Smart (1971) estimated the plasma corticosterone of adult male rats whose mothers had been either adequately fed or underfed during pregnancy and lactation. Blood was taken from some rats immediately after removal from their home cages, to establish baseline concentrations, and from others fifteen minutes after they had been placed in a situation where they had previously experienced electric shock. It is well known that stressful stimulation causes a marked rise in corticosterone output. The two groups did not differ when tested undisturbed, but after stressful stimulation corticosterone concentrations were higher in the controls than in the previously undernourished animals. The implications for behavior of this sort of difference are still largely a matter for conjecture, though there may be some clue among recent investigations of the influence of pituitary and adrenal hormones on avoidance behavior (reviewed by Levine 1971). Rats learn readily to move from one side of a box to the other on hearing a tone, when this enables them to avoid an electric shock. When the tone is subsequently presented without any succeeding shock, the frequency of avoidance responses declines; that is, there is extinction of the response. De Wied (1969) concluded from a series of experiments that ACTH inhibits extinction of avoidance responding; glucocorticosteroids have the opposite effect. Similarly, rats injected with ACTH are abnormally inhibited in a passive avoidance situation (Levine and Jones 1965). Hence, behavioral over-reaction to unpleasant stimulation may be due to a change in the hypothalamus-pituitary-adrenal system.

(iv) *Learning Ability*. A question often asked is: does early undernourishment affect intelligence? To attempt an answer, the question needs to be more precise. As it stands, it presupposes a great many things; for example, that differences in performance on a test of 'learning ability' reflect only differences in intelligence, and that differences on one test will correlate positively with those on another. Neither of these assumptions is warranted.

The usual measures of 'learning ability', namely time and error scores or number of attempts required for a certain level of performance, are of limited value in so far as they ignore most of what the animal is doing. Moreover, the aspects of behavior discussed in earlier sections probably all influence such scores. It seems that rats which have been nutritionally deprived early in life have a greater than normal hunger drive; that is, in an apparently equivalent state of deprivation, they have a stronger tendency to perform a response for food. Hence, the motivational states of normal and early underfed animals have probably not been the same in experimental situations in which they have been required to develop a habit for food reward. In view of the evidence which suggests that for any task there is an optimum internal deficit (discussed by Barnett 1972), there must always be the suspicion that one group is in a more appropriate state of deficit than the other. Likewise, it would not be surprising to find disagreement among the results from investigations employing different levels of deprivation. In tests which are dependent on punishment of incorrect responses rather than reward of correct ones, the differing responsiveness of normal and early-deprived animals to unpleasant stimulation is an uncontrolled variable of the utmost importance.

Correlations between performance in different learning situations are notoriously poor. Animals which do well on one test are not necessarily good at another. Tryon (1940) bred rats for their ability to run a maze in the dark. Eight generations of selection produced distinct 'dull' and 'bright' strains. In a later, very detailed investigation of the same strains, 'dull' rats proved equal to or better than 'bright' in three out of five measures of learning ability (Searle 1949).

There is, in any case, no consistent trend in the effects of early nutritional deprivation on performance in learning tests. The balance of evidence tips slightly in favour of the adequately fed animals, in that their performance has been significantly better rather more often than that of poorly-fed animals (reviewed by Smart 1973). In situations where the animal has to make some movement to avoid an electric shock, the modal result has been no difference. Trial-and-error learning to escape from water has been accomplished better by normal animals in some investigations, and by early deprived animals in others. For instance, Howard and Granoff (1968) found that mice undernourished in the suckling period were more efficient than controls at making a delayed response to gain access to an escape route from water. Likewise, tests with food as the reward have given rise to differences in both directions. Surprisingly, water reward has seldom been used. Recently, however, Simonson and Chow (1970) found that the offspring of underfed mother rats never became as efficient as normal progeny at running a maze for water, even after prolonged training.

The equivocal nature of these results supports the contention that normal and previously underfed animals do not learn best under the same experimental conditions: what is optimal for one, is not so for the other. Presumably, motivational and environmental circumstances have in some studies fortuitously favoured the nutritionally deprived group. These considerations lead to some refinement of the original question. It can now be couched: 'Are early undernourished animals *capable* of learning as efficiently as well-fed controls?' To solve this problem, adaptive behavior must be investigated under a variety of motivational and environmental conditions. A further need is to record more than the usual time or error scores, and to seek the underlying causes of the differences found.

(b) *Magnitude of Effect and Characteristics of Nutritional Deprivation*

Till now, experimenters have been concerned with establishing whether or not there is any consistent effect on behavior of early nutritional deprivation, rather than studying the outcome of varying the characteristics of the deprivation. The few comparative studies which have been attempted have necessarily been restricted to only a few of the many permutations of type, severity, timing and duration of dietary restriction.

The controversy over the relative effects of low protein and low calorie diets is unresolved. There is no good evidence of any difference in behavior between the offspring of mother rats fed one or the other diet. When the experimental treatment is applied after weaning, the usual procedure is to feed one group a diet deficient in protein, and another group a quantity of good quality diet sufficient only to maintain growth at the same rate as the low-protein group. Both groups are deprived for the same length of time and then allowed free access to the good diet. Despite the equivalence of growth stunting during the deprivation period, the low-protein animals are, at that time, lethargic and appear less well than their undernourished counterparts, and during rehabilitation they tend to grow rather more slowly. This may go some way towards explaining the occasional reports of greater behavioral differences due to protein malnutrition than to calorie restriction after weaning. The difference may be in the effective severity of growth stunting rather than the diet *per se*.

The timing of the nutritional insult with respect to the animal's developmental schedule is probably important. If food shortage is experienced late in development, then the effects on behavior are minimal. The behavior of pigs malnourished from three weeks of age is more aberrant than that of pigs fed the same low protein diet for the same length of time but from seven weeks (Barnes *et al.* 1970). If rats have experienced food restriction during or shortly after the suckling period, they have a stronger tendency to hoard food than rats deprived later in life (reviewed by Bronfenbrenner 1968). It is, as yet, impossible to say whether nutritional deprivation which precedes the main part of the brain growth-spurt has less influence than deprivation which spans the peak. There are reports of changed behavior in the rat (whose brain growth-spurt is postnatal) resulting from nutritional deprivation of mothers in pregnancy (Caldwell and Churchill 1967, Simonson *et al.* 1971). But it should be borne in mind that different aspects of behavior may be most susceptible to environmental influence at different stages in development.

It is probably true to say that the longer the period of dietary restriction, the greater its effect, as long as it does not occur late in development. Rats poorly fed from birth till seven weeks of age behave more abnormally than animals underfed in the three-week suckling period alone (Fraňková and Barnes 1968*b*). The effects of undernourishing mother rats in pregnancy and lactation are additive with respect to certain aspects of their progeny's behavior (see Figs. 5 and 6 of this chapter, and Smart (1971)). Another dimension is added by the remarkable findings of Cowley and Griesel (1966) on the effects of chronic protein malnutrition. For two generations, rats received only a diet moderately low in protein. Feeding the second generation rats a good quality diet from weaning, and retaining both them and their offspring on the better diet, did not eliminate all the effects of the ancestral malnutrition. The offspring were somewhat slow in development, and made more errors than controls in running a maze for food. No matter how this observation is interpreted, the maternal effect stands. Its implications are far-reaching.

Summary and Conclusions

There is unequivocal evidence of delayed neurological maturation resulting from nutritional deprivation at the time of the brain growth-spurt. Whether previously undernourished animals have a reduced capacity for learning new habits is uncertain. Motivational artefacts probably contribute to the confusion among the results. However, there is consistent evidence of lasting effects on other aspects of behavior. Decreased activity in novel surroundings, overreaction to stressful stimulation, and heightened responsiveness to food when hungry, are all typical of adult animals which have experienced nutritional deprivation early in life. The magnitude of these effects seems to depend on the severity, duration and timing of the nutritional insult, though the last is not yet established with any precision.

The evidence for lasting *structural* changes in the brain related to the timing of the undernutrition is clearer. The brain growth-spurt is not the only period of development when ultimate structure can be modified by these means, but it is by far the most vulnerable period in crude terms of quantitative ultimate achievement and measurable physical distortion. There is some evidence from studies of human growth and development, even in privileged communities, which seems to resemble the physical findings in animals (Davies and Davis 1970); moreover, some of the (as yet) scanty behavioral data from the un-privileged world do support the idea that children can be permanently affected by malnutrition in their early years (Cravioto and DeLicardie 1970, Chase and Martin 1970). Indeed, the correspondence is close between the vulnerable period for human behavioral development and the human brain growth-spurt. However, it must be remembered that in all developmental findings such correspondence can as easily be coincidental as meaningful.

Perhaps it would not be stretching the evidence too far to say that in the light of present knowledge there is a period of human development, extending from the second trimester of gestation well into the second postnatal year, when the brain appears to have a once-only opportunity to grow properly. It is, at this time, especially important that children should grow at a proper rate, under the best conditions. Amongst these environmental factors, nutrition is central to proper growth, a restriction in which may well have lasting behavioral consequences.

Acknowledgements. Our work is supported by a grant from the Medical Research Council. We are also grateful to the National Fund for Research into Crippling Diseases and the Spastics Society for their help. We especially thank our colleagues, Dr. B. P. F. Adlard and Miss J. Sands for their continuing collaboration.

REFERENCES

Adlard, B. P. F., Dobbing, J. (1971a) 'Vulnerability of developing brain. III. Development of four enzymes in the brains of normal and undernourished rats.' *Brain Research.*, **28**, 97.
—— —— (1971b) 'Phosphofructokinase and fumarate hydratase in developing rat brain.' *Journal of Neurochemistry*, **18**, 1299.
—— —— (1971c) 'Elevated acetylcholinesterase activity in adult rat brain after undernutrition in early life.' *Brain Research*, **30**, 198.
—— Smart, J. L. (1971) 'Plasma 11-hydroxycorticosteroid concentrations in stressed adult rats after undernutrition in early life.' *Biochemical Journal*, **125**, 12P.
Altman, J. (1970) 'Postnatal neurogenesis and the problem of neural plasticity.' *in* Himwich, W. A. (Ed.) *Developmental Neurobiology.* Springfield, Ill.: C. C. Thomas. p. 197.
—— Sudarshan, K., Das, G. D., McCormick, N., Barnes, D. (1971) 'The influence of nutrition on neural and behavioral development. III. Development of some motor, particularly locomotor patterns during infancy.' *Developmental Psychobiology*, **4**, 97.
Baird, A., Widdowson, E. M., Cowley, J. J. (1971) 'Effects of calorie and protein deficiencies early in life on the subsequent learning ability of rats.' *British Journal of Nutrition*, **25**, 391.
Barnes, R. H., Neely, C. S., Kwong, E., Labadan, B. A., Fraňková, S. (1968) 'Postnatal nutritional deprivations as determinants of adult rat behavior towards food, its consumption and utilization.' *Journal of Nutrition*, **96**, 467.
—— Moore, A. U., Pond, W. G. (1970) 'Behavioral abnormalities in young adult pigs caused by malnutrition in early life.' *Journal of Nutrition*, **100**, 149.

Barnett, S. A. (1963) *A Study in Behaviour*. London: Methuen.

—— Burn, J. (1967) 'Early stimulation and maternal behaviour.' *Nature (London)*, **213**, 150.

—— Smart, J. L., Widdowson, E. M. (1971) 'Early nutrition and the activity and feeding of rats in an artificial environment.' *Developmental Psychobiology*, **4**, 1.

Benstead, J. P. M., Dobbing, J., Morgan, R. S., Reid, R. T. W., Payling Wright, G. (1957) 'Neurological development and myelination in the spinal cord of the chick embryo.' *Journal of Embryology and Experimental Morphology*, **5**, 428.

Boulouard, R. (1963) 'Effect of cold and starvation on adrenocortical activity of rats.' *Federation Proceedings*, **22**, 750.

Brett, E. (1965) 'The estimation of foetal maturity by the neurological examination of the neonate.' *in* Dawkins, M., MacGregor, W. G. (Eds.) *Gestational Age, Size and Maturity*. Clinics in Developmental Medicine, No, 19. London: Spastics Society with Heinemann. p. 105.

Bronfenbrenner, U. (1968) 'Early deprivation in mammals and man.' *in* Newton, G., Levine, S. (Eds.) *Early Experience and Behavior*. Springfield, Ill.: C. C. Thomas. p. 629.

Caldwell, D. F., Churchill, J. A. (1967) 'Learning ability in the progeny of rats administered a protein-deficient diet during the second half of gestation.' *Neurology (Minneapolis)*, **17**, 95.

Chase, H. P., Martin, H. P. (1970) 'Undernutrition and child development.' *New England Journal of Medicine*, **282**, 933.

Chow, B. F., Blackwell, R. Q., Blackwell, B., Hou, T. Y., Anilane, J. K., Sherwin, R. W. (1968) 'Maternal nutrition and metabolism of the offspring: studies in rats and man.' *American Journal of Public Health*, **58**, 668.

Cowley, J. J., Griesel, R. D. (1963) 'The development of second generation low protein rats.' *Journal of Genetic Psychology*, **103**, 233.

—— —— (1966) 'The effect on growth and behaviour of rehabilitating first and second generation low protein rats.' *Animal Behaviour*, **14**, 506.

Cravioto, J., DeLicardie, E. R. (1970) 'Mental performance in school age children. Findings after recovery from early severe malnutrition.' *American Journal of Diseases of Children*, **120**, 404.

Davies, P. A., Davis, J. P. (1970) 'Very low birth-weight and subsequent head growth.' *Lancet*, **ii**, 1216.

Davison, A. N., Peters, A. (1970) *Myelination*. Springfield, Ill.: C. C. Thomas.

Dickerson, J. W. T., Dobbing, J. (1966) 'Some peculiarities of cerebellar growth.' *Proceedings of the Royal Society of Medicine*, **59**, 1088.

—— —— (1967) 'Prenatal and postnatal growth and development of the central nervous system of the pig.' *Proceedings of the Royal Society B.*, **166**, 384

Dobbing, J. (1968*a*) 'Vulnerable periods in developing brain.' *in* Davison, A. N., Dobbing, J. (Eds.) *Applied Neurochemistry*. Oxford: Blackwell. p. 287.

—— (1968*b*) 'Effects of experimental undernutrition on development of the nervous system.' *in* Scrimshaw, N. S., Gordon, J. E. (Eds.) *Malnutrition, Learning and Behavior*. Boston: M.I.T. Press. p. 181.

—— (1970) 'Undernutrition and the developing brain: the relevance of animal models to the human problem.' *American Journal of Diseases of Children*, **120**, 411.

—— Sands, J. (1970*a*) 'Growth and development of the brain and spinal cord of the guinea pig.' *Brain Research*, **17**, 115.

—— —— (1970*b*) 'Timing of neuroblast multiplication in developing human brain.' *Nature (London)*, **226**, 639.

—— —— (1972*a*) 'Vulnerability of developing brain. IX. The effect of nutritional growth retardation on the timing of the brain growth-spurt.' *Biology of the Neonate*, **19**, 363.

—— —— (1972*b*) 'Growth and development of the human brain.' (In preparation.)

—— Hopewell, J. W., Lynch, A. (1971) 'Vulnerability of developing brain. VII. Permanent deficit of neurons in cerebral and cerebellar cortex following early mild undernutrition.' *Experimental Neurology*, **32**, 439.

Fraňková, S. (1971) 'Relationship between nutrition during lactation and maternal behaviour of rats.' *Activitas Nervosa Superior (Praha)*, **13**, 1.

—— Barnes, R. H. (1968*a*) 'Influence of malnutrition in early life on exploratory behavior of rats.' *Journal of Nutrition*, **96**, 477.

Fraňková, S., Barnes, R. H. (1968*b*) 'Effect of malnutrition in early life on avoidance conditioning and behavior of adult rats.' *Journal of Nutrition*, **96**, 485.

Guthrie, H. A. (1968) 'Severe undernutrition in early infancy and behavior in rehabilitated albino rats.' *Physiology and Behavior*, **3**, 619.

Howard, E., Granoff, D. M. (1968) 'Effect of neonatal food restriction in mice on brain growth, DNA and cholesterol and on adult delayed response learning.' *Journal of Nutrition*, **95**, 111.

Hunt, J. M. (1941) 'The effects of infant feeding-frustration upon adult hoarding in the albino rat.' *Journal of Abnormal and Social Psychology*, **36**, 338.

Lee, C. J., Chow, B. F. (1965) 'Protein metabolism in the offspring of underfed mother rats.' *Journal of Nutrition*, **87**, 439.

Levine, S. (1971) 'Stress and behavior.' *Scientific American*, **224**, (1), 26.

—— Jones, L. E. (1965) 'Adrenocorticotropic hormone (ACTH) and passive avoidance learning.' *Journal of Comparative and Physiological Psychology*, **59**, 357.

Levitsky, D. A., Barnes, R. H. (1970) 'Effect of early malnutrition on the reaction of adult rats to aversive stimuli.' *Nature (London)*, **225**, 468.

Michaelis, R., Schulte, F. J., Nolte, R. (1970) 'Motor behavior of small for gestational age newborn infants.' *Journal of Pediatrics*, **76**, 208.

Platt, B. S., Stewart, R. J. C. (1968) 'Effect of protein-calorie deficiency on dogs. I. Reproduction, growth, and behaviour.' *Developmental Medicine and Child Neurology*, **10**, 3.

Robinson, R. J. (1966) 'Assessment of gestational age by neurological examination.' *Archives of Disease in Childhood*, **41**, 437.

Searle, L. V. (1949) 'The organization of hereditary maze-brightness and maze-dullness. *Genetic Psychology Monographs*, **39**, 279.

Seitz, P. F. D. (1954) 'The effects of infantile experiences upon adult behavior in animal subjects. I. Effects of litter size during infancy upon adult behavior in the rat.' *American Journal of Psychiatry*, **110**, 916.

Simonson, M., Chow, B. F. (1970) 'Maze studies on progeny of underfed mother rats.' *Journal of Nutrition*, **100**, 685.

—— Sherwin, R. W., Anilane, J. K., Yu, W. Y., Chow, B. F. (1969) 'Neuromotor development in progeny of underfed mother rats.' *Journal of Nutrition*, **98**, 18.

—— Stephan, J. K., Hanson, H. M., Chow, B. F. (1971) 'Open field studies in offspring of underfed mother rats.' *Journal of Nutrition*, **101**, 331.

Smart, J. L. (1971) 'An experimental investigation of the effect of early nutritional deprivation on behaviour.' *in Proceedings of the XIIIth Congress of Pediatrics*, Vienna, Vol. 2, 65.

—— (1973) 'Long-lasting effects of early nutritional deprivation on behaviour.' *in* Dobbing, J. (Ed.) *Undernutrition and Developing Brain*. London: Saunders. (In preparation.)

—— Dobbing, J. (1971*a*) 'Vulnerability of developing brain. II. Effects of early nutritional deprivation on reflex ontogeny and development of behaviour in the rat.' *Brain Research*, **28**, 85.

—— —— (1971*b*) 'Vulnerability of developing brain. VI. Relative effects of fetal and early postnatal undernutrition on reflex ontogeny and development of behaviour in the rat.' *Brain Research*, **33**, 303.

—— —— (1972) 'Vulnerability of developing brain. IV. Passive avoidance behavior in young rats following maternal undernutrition.' *Developmental Psychobiology*, **5**, 129.

Souza, S. W. de, Dobbing, J. (1971) 'Cerebral edema in developing brain. I. Normal water and cation content in developing rat brain and postmortem changes.' *Experimental Neurology*, **32**, 431.

Tryon, R. C. (1940) 'Genetic differences in maze-learning ability in rats.' *Yearbook of the National Society for Studies in Education*, **39**, 111.

Widdowson, E. M., McCance, R. A. (1963) 'The effect of finite periods of undernutrition at different ages on the composition and subsequent development of the rat.' *Proceedings of the Royal Society B.*, **158**, 329.

Wied, D.de (1969) 'Effects of peptide hormones on behavior.' *in* Ganong, W. F., Martini, L. (Eds.) *Frontiers in Neuroendocrinology*. New York: O.U.P. p. 97.

Winick, M., Noble, A. (1966) 'Cellular response in rats during malnutrition at various ages.' *Journal of Nutrition*, **89**, 300.

—— Fish, I., Rosso, P. (1968) 'Cellular recovery in rat tissues after a brief period of neonatal malnutrition.' *Journal of Nutrition*, **95**, 623.

Zeman, F. J. (1967) 'Effects on the young rat of maternal protein restriction.' *Journal of Nutrition*, **93**, 167.

CHAPTER 3

Early Experience and Susceptibility to Disease: the Case of Gastric Erosions

ROBERT ADER

One of the common hazards of biological research is individual variation of unknown origin. This is very evident in the general area of research on 'stress'. The prominence of individual variation has led to the hypothesis that previous individual experience is of paramount importance in determining responses to adverse stimulation. In psychology, this, among other factors, has led to intensive research on the effects of early experience, both on subsequent behavior and on resistance to 'stress'. In the medical literature, too, there is a growing awareness of the influence of individual differences in determining susceptibility to disease. Indeed, a major question in psychosomatic medicine is why, when exposed to similar pathogens, some individuals become ill and others do not; and what determines the 'choice' of disease. The writings of Dubos (1959) emphasise this with a plea for the recognition of the rôle of social and other environmental factors in the genesis of organic disease.

For the past several years my colleagues and I have been studying 'psychosomatic' phenomena in laboratory animals. More specifically, we have been concerned with the effects of early experience, including prenatal influences, on (i) developmental processes, (ii) subsequent behavior and physiological reactivity, and, ultimately, (iii) susceptibility to a variety of diseases (reviewed by Ader 1970a). Social stimulation during development has been clearly shown to influence susceptibility to disease. Such results are entirely consistent with the concept of multiple causation of illness (Engel 1962). The use of laboratory rats and mice in such research allows direct tests of hypotheses on social and physiological interactions responsible for the readiness with which a disease is developed. With animals, it is possible to investigate how simple experiences affect individual development, how experience becomes translated into altered physiological states, and how these states influence response to pathogenic stimuli.

The features of early life that we have studied experimentally include direct stimulation in infancy (daily handling or electric shock, for example), and the mother-young relationship (varying the age at which animals are weaned, brief separation from the mother, and so on). The social environment of older animals may be modified by housing them either in groups or alone. Diseases or potential pathogens studied include alloxan diabetes, carcinogens, viral agents, *Plasmodium berghei* (a rodent malaria), X-irradiation, audiogenic seizures, electroconvulsive shock, a conflict situation, and physical immobilization.

Lest I be accused of overstating the case for the effects of early life experiences, it should be made clear that such experiences as have been studied do not influence the individual's response to all disease. Premature weaning, for example, influences the incidence of rumenal ulcers in a conflict situation (Ader 1962) and also mortality due to a transplanted tumor (Ader and Friedman 1965a), but early separation from the mother does not affect susceptibility to immobilization-induced gastric erosions. Similarly, handling infant rats and mice affects resistance to a transplanted tumor (Ader and Friedman 1965b), a transplanted murine leukemia (Levine and Cohen 1959), electroconvulsive shock (Levine 1962), and immobilization-induced gastric lesions (Ader 1965), but we have unpublished findings indicating no effect on susceptibility to alloxan diabetes, a viral disease, or the spontaneous development of leukemia in a genetically predisposed strain of mice.

Moreover, the differential effects of early experiences on disease susceptibility are not always in the same direction. Handling during the pre-weaning period increases resistance to gastric erosions, and retards the rate of growth of a transplanted tumor, but decreases resistance to a transplanted leukemia and to electroconvulsive shock. Finally, the effects of various kinds of stimulation during early life are not necessarily the same. For example, differences in the behavior of handled, shocked, and unmanipulated control animals may depend upon what kinds of behavior are being measured. Handled animals are more resistant to gastric lesions that either shocked or unmanipulated animals; the last two do not differ. When stimulation is experienced during the first ten days of life, the mortality rate to a transplanted tumor is decreased in handled and shocked animals, but stimulation throughout the twenty-one day pre-weaning period decreases mortality rate only in shocked animals. In short, whether the incidence of disease is influenced, and the direction of any effect observed, depend on both the type of manipulation (that is, the changes induced by the early experience) and also the nature of the disease (that is, the changes elicited by the pathogenic stimulus). The interaction between these determines disease susceptibility.

Our general approach is outlined in Figure 1. Potentially pathogenic stimuli do not act in a vacuum; they are superimposed upon a psychophysiological state, which is determined, in part, by the history of the organism, including, particularly, early life experiences. Similarly, the effects of early life experiences are, themselves, superimposed upon a background of psychophysiological reactivity, determined by prenatal and genetical factors. Not only is it possible for all these factors to interact, but this interaction takes place within a social and cultural environment which also contributes to the ultimate expression of the phenotype. What an experimenter observes or measures, then, is a function of both the stimulus and his measuring instrument—in this case, a living organism.

To illustrate the influence of early experience, I describe here a series of studies of experimentally-induced gastric lesions in the rat. Susceptibility to gastric lesions has been a particularly good model for the study of psycho-

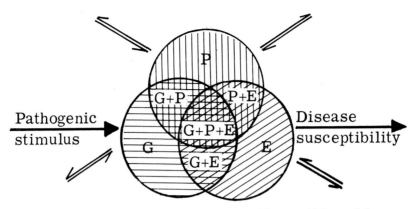

SOCIAL ENVIRONMENT

Pathogenic stimulus

Disease susceptibility

P

G+P   P+E

G+P+E

G   E

G+E

Fig. 1. Schematic representation of interactions of factors which may influence susceptibility to disease. P = prenatal environment, G = genotype, and E = early postnatal environment.

somatic phenomena in animals. It is a good model not only because the lesions induced experimentally bear a striking similarity to the disease in man, or because the physiological mechanisms hypothesized to mediate the pathology in man and rat have common features; it is a good model because gastric erosion is a pathological process to which the rat is liable, and which is demonstrably sensitive to the influence of genetical and experiential manipulations and to the interaction between psychological and physiological variables. These interactions have been directly studied in experiments designed to determine the effects of early life experiences and differential housing on susceptibility to gastric erosions in animals biologically predisposed to the development of gastric lesions (Ader 1970*b*). First, however, let me provide the background for this research.

Plasma Pepsinogen and Human Duodenal Ulcer

People with duodenal ulcer have higher plasma pepsinogen levels than patients without gastro-intestinal pathology (Mirsky 1958). Moreover, the level of plasma pepsinogen is a measure of gastric secretory potential, and predicts susceptibility to duodenal ulcer (Weiner *et al.* 1957, Yessler *et al.* 1959). The distribution of plasma pepsinogen levels shown in Figure 2 was obtained from a large population of young men on induction into the Army. Individuals with levels within the highest and lowest fifteen per cent of the population were selected for intensive study, including psychological tests. Those that developed duodenal ulcers during their basic training came from the segment of the population with the highest plasma pepsinogen levels.

As these investigators pointed out, however, the relationship between pepsinogen level and the onset of ulceration is not simple. High plasma

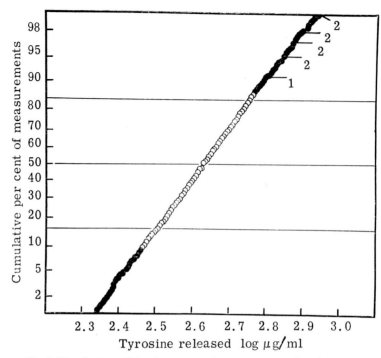

Fig. 2. Distribution of blood serum pepsinogen concentrations in a group of Army recruits. The frequency distribution of the logarithm of the concentration of pepsinogen is plotted on a probit scale. The subjects selected for special study were among those designated by solid circles. The numerals refer to individuals that developed duodenal ulcer. (*From* Weiner *et al.* 1957).

pepsinogen is neither necessary nor sufficient for the development of ulcers; although it is correlated with the development of ulceration, it represents only one variable in a complex interaction of the individual's adaptive capacity and the demands of his social environment. Conditions are optimal for the manifestation of duodenal ulcer if: (i) there is a high plasma pepsinogen level (representing a 'biological predisposition'); (ii) the personality structure is such that some change in the environment is perceived as 'stressful'; (iii) the individual is unable to cope successfully with this environment. Presumably, the individual's perception of, and ability to cope with, environmental demands are determined, at least in part, by early experience.

Plasma Pepsinogen and Gastric Erosions in Rats

The relationship between plasma pepsinogen and the gastro-intestinal pathology of the laboratory rat is in many ways similar to that of man. A rat subjected to a period of physical immobilization plus food and water deprivation often develops erosions in the glandular portion of the stomach (Fig. 3). As with human duodenal ulcer, animals with gastric erosions due to physical restraint have higher pepsinogen levels than those that have not developed

40

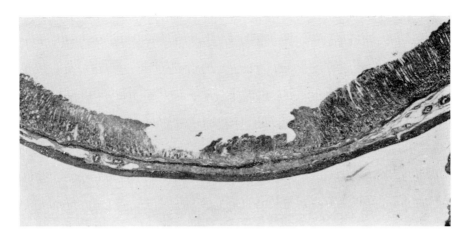

Fig. 3. Photomicrographs of a gastric lesion in the glandular portion of the stomach of a rat (upper × 30, lower × 60). (*From* Ader *et al.* 1960.)

41

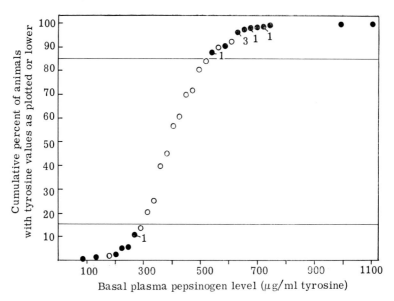

Fig. 4. Cumulative percentage frequency distribution of basal plasma pepsinogen levels of 285 male rats. The solid circles represent the pepsinogen levels of animals selected for six hours of immobilization. The numerals refer to animals that developed gastric erosions. (*From* Ader 1963.)

lesions (Ader *et al.* 1960). Moreover, the basal plasma pepsinogen level of rats can be used to predict susceptibility to gastric erosions induced by immobilization (Ader 1963).

In a study analogous to that made on man, plasma pepsinogen was determined in a large population of rats. Rats with values falling within the highest and lowest fifteen per cent of the distribution were selected for further study (Fig. 4). Animals with high plasma pepsinogen were found to be more likely to develop gastric erosions than those with low values. This relationship, however, holds only for animals subjected to immobilization for six hours. This period is about the lowest which leads to the development of gastric lesions. Hence there is an interaction between pepsinogen level and the severity of the 'stress'. Furthermore, not all animals with high plasma pepsinogen levels develop erosions; nor do all animals with low pepsinogen levels escape erosions.

What could account for the variation in response? For human populations it can be argued that what is 'stressful' for one individual is not so for another—that different individuals perceive and respond differently to the same conditions. Such differences are, presumably, determined in part by differences in personal histories. There is evidence that the same applies to rats.

Among the many possible contributory factors, one was the fluctuating internal state reflected in the daily rhythm of activity. Accordingly, one population of rats was immobilized for six hours just before the peak of their most active phase; another group was similarly restrained when they would have been

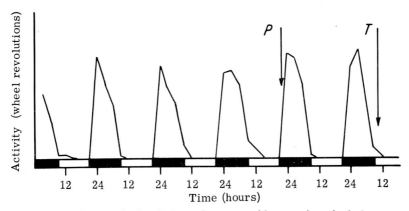

Fig. 5. Activity record of a single rat in a cage with a running wheel. Arrows indicate the times at which such an animal would be immobilized at the beginning of the peak (P) or at the trough (T) of its activity rhythm. (*From* Ader 1967*a*.)

least active (Fig. 5). It was hypothesized that animal s immobilized at the peak of their daily activity rhythm would respond to the restraint more than animals immobilized during the trough; they would therefore be more susceptible to gastric erosions. This was confirmed (Ader 1964, 1967*a*). Clearly, then, the internal state upon which potentially pathogenic stimulation is superimposed is critical in determining the individual's response. This finding also has a methodological implication: it emphasizes the importance of testing animals at the same time each day.

Effects of Prenatal and Early Postnatal Experience

I now turn to effects of early experience. The kinds of stimulation used include electric shock or simply handling the infant animal. A handled pup is removed from the nest, and held in one hand for three minutes every day from birth until the animal is weaned at twenty-one days. Later, the social environment may be varied by caging the animals either alone or in groups of like-sex peers.

The social environment is an extremely important variable. Whether it has an effect and, if so, the direction in which group-housed animals differ from those kept alone, depends upon the disease (Ader 1967*b*). With respect to gastric erosions, group-housed rats are generally more susceptible to the effects of restraint than solitary animals (Stern *et al.* 1960, Ader 1965, Sines 1965). Once again, we see the importance of controlling every possible environmental variable, if repeatable results are to be obtained.

As noted above, handling infant animals has an effect on the adult organism's susceptibility to somatic disease, and the direction in which handled animals differ from non-handled animals (or animals subjected to other kinds of manipulations during infancy) depends upon the disease (Ader 1970*a*). Handling during early life increases resistance to gastric lesions induced by immobilization (Table I).

TABLE I
Effects of early experience (handling) on incidence of gastric erosions in rats subjected to immobilization

Source	Strain	Days of stimulation	Rats per cage	Hours of restraint	Animals with gastric erosions Handled (per cent)	Control (per cent)
Weininger (1956)	Wistar	21 to 41	1	48	0.56*	3.38*
Winokur et al. (1959)	Sprague-Dawley	23 to 43	15	48	22.5	67.0
Ader (1965)	Heterogeneous	1 to 21	5 or 6	18	66.7	80.8
		1 to 21	1	18	42.8	80.0
Ader (unpublished)	Charles River (CD)	1 to 10 21 to 30	1	18	0.0	27.5
McMichael (1966)	Sprague-Dawley	1 to 22	2	57 to 65	33.3	55.5

*Mean number of bleeding points per animal

The earliest systematic observations were made by Weininger (1956), who 'gentled' (handled) rats for ten minutes each day for three weeks after weaning. At maturity, the handled animals and non-handled litter mates were immobilized for forty-eight hours. Handled animals suffered less haemorrhagic damage to the gastro-intestinal system than did controls. Winokur et al. (1959) obtained similar results with rats handled daily for five or ten minutes. There were no differences between the two handled groups, but both were more resistant to gastric erosions than non-handled controls.

Studies in my laboratory have confirmed these findings (Table 1). Two strains of rats were used, differing in the readiness with which they develop gastric erosions. Rats of both strains, handled before or after weaning, developed fewer erosions (Ader 1965)—at least under these periods of immobilization.

An especially interesting finding concerns the interaction between early handling and housing (Ader 1965). Rats were subjected to daily handling or electric shock or remained unmanipulated throughout the pre-weaning period. After weaning, half of each group was housed individually, and half was group-housed. At maturity, the animals were tested for their response to handling (Ader and Friedman 1964). In this test, the group-housed rats were caged individually on the preceding day. The experimenter simply reached into each cage, touched, and then attempted to pick up each animal. The incidence of startle responses, vocalization, and resistance to being picked up were recorded on an all-or-none basis. The rats that had been housed in groups were less reactive than those housed alone. Among the group-housed animals, there were no differences between the handled, shocked, and control groups. Among the individually housed animals, however, handling did result in a reduction of reactivity. These same animals were subsequently trained to avoid electric shock in a shuttle box situation. Learning to avoid shock was similarly influenced by the interaction of early experience and housing: differences between the handled, shocked, and control animals were observed only among those that had been individually housed. The animals were then immobilized, and the same

44

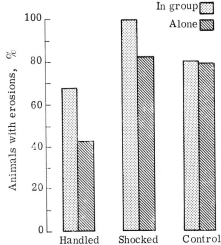

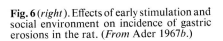

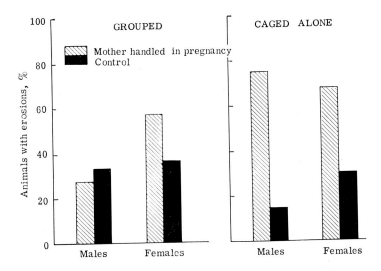

Fig. 6 (*right*). Effects of early stimulation and social environment on incidence of gastric erosions in the rat. (*From* Ader 1967*b*.)

Fig. 7 (*below*). Effects of prenatal maternal handling and later social environment on incidence of gastric erosions in rats. (*From* Ader and Plaut 1968.)

interaction was again observed. The difference in the incidence of erosions between differentially manipulated animals was greater among those housed individually (Fig. 6).

Going back further in the life history, Ader and Plaut (1968) handled pregnant rats throughout gestation. The offspring of these rats, and of non-handled controls, were fostered at birth on to non-handled lactating females. This eliminated the effects of postnatal maternal influences. After weaning, half the offspring of each class were housed in groups and half were caged alone. All were tested behaviorally at maturity. They were then immobilized, and the incidence of gastric erosions was determined. The results revealed an interaction between prenatal maternal handling and the later social environment (Fig. 7). As with postnatal manipulation, housing animals in groups reduced or eliminated differences between the experimental animals and the controls. Differences were observed between the two populations of individually caged rats: the offspring of females handled during gestation were *more* susceptible to immobilization-induced gastric erosions than were controls.

Practical considerations aside, such results suggest that behavioral and physiological processes—including disease susceptibility—can be influenced by experiences occurring early in life, and that such effects are capable of being modified by subsequent environmental events. Conversely, environmental factors, in this instance differential housing, evidently can bring about behavioral and physiological changes in the organism which are determined, in part, by the psychophysiological background upon which that form of environmental stimulation is superimposed.

Selective Breeding

Rats of the Sprague-Dawley strain can be selectively bred for susceptibility to gastric lesions (Sines 1959). The lesions can be detected, without killing the animals, by illuminating the stomachs after distending them with injected air. Sines (1961) used rats that developed lesions under restraint for selective breeding; there was a progressive increase in the tendency to develop lesions over five generations. The selected population has now been maintained for more than twenty generations. Breeding of the lesion-susceptible population, however, results in smaller litters than usual. The females have difficulty in delivering litters, and often fail to care adequately for the pups that are born (Sines 1961, 1963).

Sines (1961) has described his lesion-susceptible rats as more 'emotionally reactive' than normal Sprague-Dawley animals. This statement is based on behavior observed in an 'open-field' situation. Accordingly, Mikhail and Broadhurst (1965) hypothesized that the Maudsley 'reactive' and 'non-reactive' strains of rats, which had been selectively bred on the basis of 'emotional' defaecation scores in the open field, would differ in susceptibility to gastric erosions: the reactive strain was expected to develop more lesions in response to immobilization. But these two strains did not, in fact, differ in the number or size of the erosions which developed after thirty-six or forty-eight hours of restraint.

Ader (1967c) therefore examined the relationship between 'emotional reactivity' and lesion susceptibility in six independent, unselected populations. The findings provided no evidence for a relationship between 'emotionality' and susceptibility to gastric erosions. Evidently, the relationship observed by Sines (1961, 1962) was a concomitant of selective breeding of the particular population he used.

Consistent with this are the findings from studies, already mentioned, on prenatal and early postnatal experience: low emotional reactivity, due to particular treatment in early life, is sometimes associated with a decrease and sometimes with an increase in susceptibility to gastric lesions (Ader 1965, Ader and Plaut 1968).

Interaction of Genotype, Early Experience and Social Environment

We now had evidence of variation in the development of gastric erosions due to three groups of causes: (i) genetical, (ii) special features of the early environment, (iii) the social environment of the adult. The next step was to study further the interactions between them. Lesion-susceptible male rats were therefore mated with Charles River (CD) females—the stock animals in our colony. Sines and McDonald (1968) had demonstrated that a high level of lesion susceptibility could still be maintained in such animals. The controls were CD rats.

At parturition, entire litters (each containing ten pups) of experimental and control animals were divided at random into three groups. Members of one group were handled for three minutes each day for the twenty-one days before weaning, by holding the rat in one hand. Those of a second group were handled during the three weeks immediately after weaning. A control group was not handled at all. After weaning, all rats were group-housed until they were forty-two days old. They were then recaged, half from each of the three groups individually, and half in groups of four or five.

At three months of age, all animals were tested for their reaction to handling. As before, group-housed animals were less emotionally reactive than those caged alone. This applied both to the lesion-susceptible rats and to the controls. Differences between handled and non-handled animals were again observed only among those housed alone; handling reduced 'emotional reactivity' among the controls, but not among the lesion-susceptible animals.

One week after the behavioral tests, the plasma pepsinogen of the males was determined (Fig. 8). The pepsinogen levels of the lesion-susceptible rats proved to be higher than those of controls. Hence, in breeding for susceptibility to gastric erosions the rats had also been bred for high pepsinogen levels.

Pepsinogen levels were not influenced by the manner in which the animals were housed, but there was an interaction between genotype and early experience. That is, pepsinogen levels were influenced both by handling and by the type of rat handled. Figure 9 summarizes the findings. Pepsinogen levels of controls were highest after early handling, lowest after no handling. In contrast, handling before weaning did not result in an increase in pepsinogen in the lesion-susceptible population.

When the animals were four months old they were deprived of food and water for eighteen hours, and then immobilized in flexible wire mesh for six hours. They were then killed, and the incidence of gastric erosions in the upper, glandular portion of the stomach was determined (Ader *et al.* 1960, Ader 1963). The incidence of lesions was 56.5 per cent in the susceptible population and 19.3 per cent in the controls; the mean number of erosions per animal was 1.90 and 0.42, respectively.

Besides the difference in susceptibility between the lesion-susceptible and control populations, susceptibility to gastric erosions was determined by the early experience and the subsequent social environment of the animals. These findings (Fig. 10) are, again, identical with previous observations (Ader 1965).

47

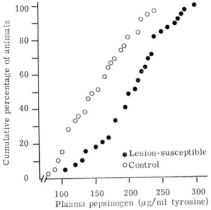

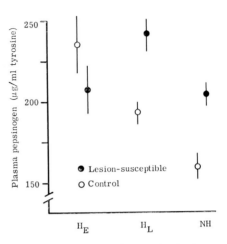

Fig. 8. Cumulative percentage frequency distribution of basal plasma pepsinogen levels in populations of lesion-susceptible and control rats. (*From* Ader 1970*b*).

Fig. 9. Plasma pepsinogen levels (mean ± S.E.) in lesion-susceptible and control rats that were not handled (NH) or subjected to handling before weaning (H$_E$) or after weaning (H$_L$). (*From* Ader 1970*b*.)

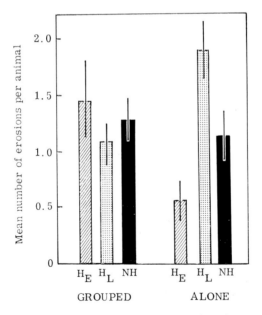

Fig. 10. Incidence of gastric erosions in non-handled (NH) rats and in animals handled before (H$_E$) or after (H$_L$) weaning as a function of social environment. Vertical bars represent standard errors of the means. (*From* Ader 1970*b*.)

Handling during early life did not influence the development of gastric erosions in animals that were subsequently housed in groups. Among the individually housed animals, however, those handled during the first three weeks of life were less susceptible to gastric erosions than non-handled animals or animals that experienced handling after weaning. Moreover, this effect of handling before weaning was the same for the control as for the lesion-susceptible population.

Summary

To summarize, the genetically susceptible population of rats was, as expected, more susceptible to immobilization-induced gastric erosions than the control population. The most notable aspect of these results, however, was that manipulation of experiences early in life could influence a genetically determined vulnerability to disease: handling experienced during the first three weeks of life decreased subsequent susceptibility to lesions regardless of the genetically determined difference between the two populations. Further, it was evidently critical that the handling be experienced during the first three weeks of life. Finally, the differences in lesion susceptibility did not parallel either experientially determined differences in emotional reactivity or experientially determined differences in plasma pepsinogen. True, there was a difference between the plasma pepsinogen levels of the unmanipulated lesion-susceptible and control populations. Nevertheless, the high pepsinogen level of the selectively bred animals does not seem to be the major factor in the susceptibility of these animals; nor is the magnitude of the difference in pepsinogen between the lesion-susceptible and control populations sufficient to account for the differences in susceptibility.

Conditions of rearing influence behavioral and physiological development, adult behavior and physiological reactivity. In addition, many experimental treatments can influence susceptibility to disease. I have concentrated here on the effects of early experience on susceptibility to gastric erosions, and on the interaction of genotype and environment in producing disease or resistance to it. Investigations of this kind show that the study of susceptibility to disease in an individual or population cannot be divorced from the experiential history, or the environment in which the individual or group is living. Similarly, practical problems of health care should not be limited to *post hoc* therapeutic measures, but must include prophylactic procedures as well. These should be based on an understanding of the rôle of events which may go back to the earliest periods of development. It is difficult to study such processes in man. Granted, there are limitations in applying findings from animal research directly to human beings, but this is outweighed by the advantages of using other species. The total life history of the animal can be regulated; conditions of rearing can be individually modified; specific genetically determined differences in vulnerability to disease can be utilized; and the ultimate incidence of a variety of disease processes can be determined. It may be expected that such research will contribute to our understanding of the mechanisms and the principles underlying the rôle of psychological factors in the pathogenesis of organic disease.

REFERENCES

Ader, R. (1962) 'Social factors affecting emotionality and resistence to diseases in animals. III. Early weaning and susceptibility to gastric ulcers in the rat. A control for nutritional factors.' *Journal of Comparative and Physiological Psychology*, **55**, 600.

—— (1963) 'Plasma pepsinogen level as a predictor of susceptibility to gastric erosion in the rat.' *Psychosomatic Medicine*, **25**, 221.

—— (1964) 'Gastric erosions in the rat: effects of immobilization at different points in the activity cycle.' *Science*, **145**, 406.

—— (1965) 'Effects of early experience and differential housing on behaviour and susceptibility to gastric erosions in the rat.' *Journal of Comparative and Physiological Psychology*, **60**, 233.

—— (1967a) 'Behavioural and physiological rhythms and the development of gastric erosions in the rat.' *Psychosomatic Medicine*, **29**, 345.

—— (1967b) 'The influence of psychological factors on disease susceptibility in animals.' *in* Conalty, M. L. (Ed.) *The Third International Symposium on the Husbandry of Laboratory Animals.* London: Academic Press.

—— (1967c) 'Emotional reactivity and susceptibility to gastric erosions.' *Psychological Reports*, **20**, 1188.

—— (1970a) 'The effects of early life experiences on developmental processes and susceptibility to disease in animals.' *in* Hill, J. P. (Ed.) *Minnesota Symposia on Child Psychology, Vol. 4.* Minneapolis: University of Minnesota Press.

—— (1970b) 'Effects of early experience and differential housing on susceptibility to gastric erosions in lesion-susceptible rats.' *Psychosomatic Medicine*, **32**, 569.

—— Friedman, S. B. (1964) 'Social factors affecting emotionality and resistance to disease in animals. IV. Differential housing, emotionality and Walker 256 carcinosarcoma in the rat.' *Psychological Reports*, **59**, 535.

—— —— (1965a) 'Social factors affecting emotionality and resistance to disease in animals. V. Early separation from the mother and responses to a transplanted tumor in the rat.' *Psychosomatic Medicine*, **27**, 119.

—— —— (1965b) 'Differential early experience and susceptibility to transplanted tumor in the rat.' *Journal of Comparative and Physiological Psychology*, **59**, 361.

—— Plaut, S. M. (1968) 'Effects of prenatal maternal handling on emotionality, plasma corticosterone levels, and susceptibility to gastric ulcers.' *Psychosomatic Medicine*, **30**, 277.

—— Beels, C. C., Tatum, R. (1960) 'Blood pepsinogen and gastric erosions in the rat.' *Psychosomatic Medicine*, **22**, 1.

Dubos, R. (1959) *Mirage of Health.* New York: Harper.

Engel, G. (1962) *Psychological Development in Health and Disease.* Philadelphia: W. B. Saunders.

Levine, S. (1962) 'The psychophysiological effects of infantile stimulation.' *in* Bliss, E. (Ed.) *Roots of Behaviour.* New York: Hoeber.

—— Cohen, C. (1959) 'Differential survival to leukemia as a function of infantile stimulation in DBA/2 mice.' *Proceedings of the Society for Experimental Biology and Medicine*, **102**, 53.

McMichael, R. E. (1966) 'Early-experience effects as a function of infant treatment and other experimental conditions.' *Journal of Comparative and Physiological Psychology*, **62**, 433.

Mikhail, A. A., Broadhurst, P. L. (1965) 'Stomach ulceration and emotionality in selected strains of rats.' *Journal of Psychosomatic Research*, **8**, 477.

Mirsky, I. A. (1958) 'Physiologic, psychologic, and social determinants in the etiology of duodenal ulcer.' *American Journal of Digestive Diseases*, **3**, 285.

Sines, J. O. (1959) 'Selective breeding for development of stomach lesions following stress in the rat.' *Journal of Comparative and Physiological Psychology*, **52**, 615.

—— (1961) 'Behavioural correlates of genetically determined susceptibility to stomach lesion development.' *Journal of Psychosomatic Research*, **5**, 120.

—— (1962) 'Strain differences on activity, emotionality, body weight, and susceptibility to stress induced stomach lesions.' *Journal of Genetic Psychology*, **101**, 209.

—— (1963) 'Physiological and behavioural characteristics of rats selectively bred for susceptibility to stomach lesion development.' *Journal of Neuropsychiatry*, **4**, 396.

—— (1965) 'Pre-stress sensory input as a non-pharmacologic method for controlling restraint-ulcer susceptibility.' *Journal of Psychosomatic Research*, **8**, 399.

—— McDonald, D. G. (1968) 'Heritability of stress-ulcer susceptibility in rats.' *Psychosomatic Medicine*, **30**, 390.

Stern, J. A., Winokur, G., Eisenstein, A., Taylor, R., Sly, M. (1960) 'The effect of group vs individual housing on behaviour and physiological responses to stress in the albino rat.' *Journal of Psychosomatic Research*, **4**, 185.

Weiner, H., Thaler, M., Reiser, M. F., Mirsky, I. A. (1957) 'Etiology of duodenal ulcer. I. Relation of specific psychological characteristics to rate of gastric secretion (serum pepsinogen).' *Psychosomatic Medicine*, **19**, 1.

Weininger, O. (1956) 'The effects of early experience on behaviour and growth characteristics.' *Journal of Comparative and Physiological Psychology*, **49, 1.**

Winokur, G., Stern, J. A., Taylor, R. (1959) 'Early handling and group housing: effect on development and response to stress in the rat.' *Journal of Psychosomatic Research*, **4**, 1.

Yessler, P. G., Reiser, M. F., Rioch, D. McK. (1959) 'Etiology of duodenal ulcer. II. Serum pepsinogen and peptic ulcer in inductees.' *Journal of the American Medical Association*, **169**, 451.

CHAPTER 4

Development of Monkeys After Varied Experiences During Infancy

GENE P. SACKETT and GERALD C. RUPPENTHAL

The conditions in which Primates are reared critically influence their later social, sexual, maternal, exploratory and other adaptive behavior. The most extreme effects follow deprivation of social and sensory input. This paper reviews studies of deprived macaque monkeys that have implications for theories of behavioral development (for general reviews, see Newton and Levine 1968). Most of the monkeys in these studies were reared in laboratory environments. Our objective is to describe differences in juvenile and adult laboratory behavior attributable to variations in mothering, relationships with agemates, and inanimate object stimulation during infancy. We also outline evidence concerning the unlearned responses of Primates, and findings that male monkeys are more severely affected by inadequate rearing experiences than females.

Rearing Conditions

The studies reviewed in this paper investigate the behavior of groups of Primates reared in conditions of differing complexity. The term complexity here refers to the amount of qualitatively different stimulation, and the degree of temporal stimulus change, available to the developing individual. In rank order, from the least to the most complex, the early rearing conditions commonly used are as follows: (i) total isolation, (ii) surrogate mothering, (iii) partial isolation, (iv) association with agemates only, (v) mother plus agemates, and (vi) feral rearing in natural or near-natural conditions. In what follows, terms such as 'isolate' and 'partial isolate' refer to conditions experienced in early life, and do not signify that the animals were isolated at the time of the observations described.

(i) Total social and partial sensory deprivation has been produced by rearing monkeys alone in enclosed cages (Fig. 1a). The sole sources of temporally varied stimulation are provided by feeding, cage maintenance, self-produced stimulation such as moving about the cage, and visually scanning the unchanging cage interior. Sometimes additional stimulation is provided. This has included rear-projected pictures, sounds, novel objects, or moving objects such as chains.

(ii) Isolated infant monkeys in some experiments have an artificial cloth-covered 'mother' object in the cage (Harlow 1958). The surrogate mother provides contact comfort for the baby, and may also be arranged to provide food (Fig. 1b).

Fig. 1. Basic rearing conditions used in studies of rhesus monkeys raised without mothers. (*a*) *Upper left.* Total isolation cage in which the infant has no physical contact with other animals and lives in a variationless, lighted, metal cage. (*b*) *Lower left.* Rearing with a cloth and a wire artificial surrogate mother. (*c*) *Upper right.* Partial isolation in which the infant is deprived of physical contact with other animals. (*d*) *Lower right.* Peer-only situation in which agemates live together in a wire cage.

(iii) In partial isolation there is less restriction than in total isolation or surrogate rearing; infant monkeys live alone in bare wire cages from which they can see and hear other monkeys and people (Fig. 1c), but there is no direct contact with other monkeys. In some studies a mother surrogate may also be available.

(iv) In a fourth condition, there is direct contact with conspecifics: groups of two to six infants live together in wire mesh cages, and can also see and hear monkeys in other cages (Fig. 1d). A variant of this procedure involves short daily interaction periods with agemates in the home cage or in some other location.

Infants raised in these four conditions are separated from their mothers at, or shortly after, birth. Early total isolates are put in enclosed cages immediately after separation and are fed by an experimenter with minimal interaction. Late total isolates spend some time in partial isolation before being completely isolated. Late total isolates, partial isolates, and infants reared only with age-mates ('peer-only') all spend the first weeks of life in a nursery. They receive intensive hand-feeding by experimenters during the first week, followed by less frequent hand-feeding. The neonate can usually find and consume food on its own by three or four weeks. Thus all monkeys separated from their mothers at birth, except early total isolates, receive extensive human contact during their first weeks, regardless of their subsequent treatment during infancy.

(v) In a fifth condition ('mother-peer'), infants are reared by their mothers; agemates are present either continuously or part of the time. In many experiments 'mother-peer' animals are reared in a playpen devised by Harlow and Harlow (1965). They live in a wire mesh cage with their mothers, but can enter a play area and interact with toys or other monkeys. Mothers cannot directly manipulate their infants when they are in the play area. In other studies, mother-peer groups are raised in gang pens, with physical interaction continually possible between all monkeys. Occasionally, an adult male is present, as well as several juveniles and adult females that do not have babies.

(vi) The last major group includes monkeys reared in their natural habitat, captured, and brought to a laboratory between two and five years of age. These feral monkeys are known to come from different ecological situations, including forest, sea coasts, towns, and cities. Consequently, although feral groups are considered to be normal controls for many studies, their rearing environments are not uniform.

Methods of Test and Measurement

Some of the research reported below involves extensive home cage study of gross motor activity, exploration and play, stereotyped motor movements, fear, and disturbance. A record is also made of the development of mother-infant and infant-infant social behavior in the home environment.

The neonatal period of a macaque (the first thirty days) is characterized by a variety of largely reflex responses. These include rooting of the mouth on almost any object, visual and auditory orienting, startle reactions to loud noises, grasping of objects in contact with the inner surface of hands or feet, vigorous orienting to 'lip-smacking' sounds, following after objects placed against the face and slowly withdrawn, clasping objects placed against the ventral body surface, extension of arms and legs on loss of support, and vigorous righting responses when placed on the back while not clutching an object (Mowbray and Cadell 1962). Most of these reflexes increase in intensity and decline in latency during the first two weeks, then either come under higher nervous control at about one month or disappear from the animal's repertoire (Milbrath 1970, Castell and Sackett 1972). These responses ensure close contact of the neonate with its mother, rapid acquisition of highly co-ordinated orienting, exploratory, and other behavior, and early maturation of learning ability (Harlow 1959). A major difference between macaque and human neonates is in the rapidity with which macaques develop skilled motor behavior and a repertoire leading to independence from the mother.

Although behavior during rearing is of interest, our major purpose is to outline behavioral effects that persist into adolescence and adulthood. It is our contention that transient rearing effects, or effects that are specific to the rearing environment but do not occur in other situations, are of little significance. Therefore, to identify important effects of early treatment, behavior at later ages must be studied.

Such later tests may be performed in large playrooms (Fig. 2), which vary in size and colour, are larger than most home cage situations, and usually contain structures for climbing, shelves, and toys. The size of the playrooms usually allows socially inadequate animals to keep away from other animals. To increase the probability of closer contact, tests have also been conducted in small dual or split cages (Fig. 2).

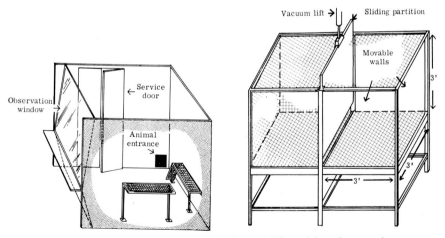

Fig. 2. Basic test situations for studying effects of differential rearing experiences. *Left*. Playroom used for studying social behavior. *Right*. One type of dual cage unit used to study non-social behavior and responses of paired animals.

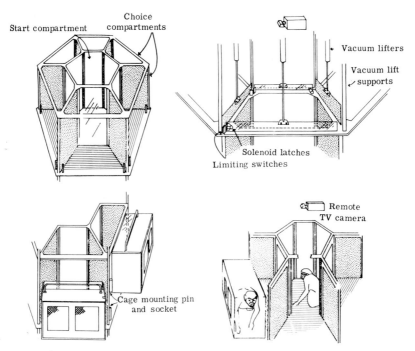

Fig. 3. The self-selection circus. *Upper left.* Central start compartment and six choice compartments. The stippled walls are opaque, and the front and inner walls are clear. *Upper right.* Vacuum cylinders for lifting inner walls, TV camera, and solenoid door latches which keep the monkey from raising doors during the trial. *Lower left.* Mounting brackets for stimulus-animal cages, which have clear glass front and top sections. *Lower right.* Relative positions of stimulus-monkey and subject during the exposure period.

Several studies reported below used a self-selection circus to measure social preferences (Fig. 3). Hexagonal, and made of metal channels, the circus contains a central start compartment, bounded by six choice compartments. Clear Plexiglas or Masonite walls slide in the channels. Behavior is viewed over closed-circuit television. In testing social preferences, stimulus animals are placed in cages attached to the outside of the choice compartments. A standard trial consists of an exposure period, with the subject in the start area and the inner Plexiglas doors between start and choice compartments closed. During this time, the subject can look through the choice compartments and see the stimulus monkeys, but cannot enter the choice areas. After exposure, the Plexiglas doors are raised, and the subject receives a period of choice, when it is free to enter and re-enter any area or to remain in the centre. Preferences are assessed by the time spent in the compartment near each stimulus monkey, and by number of entries into each compartment.

In most studies of primate development, behavior is recorded by an observer. Sets of behavioral categories have been devised from normative studies of the social development of several primate species (Altman 1965, Hansen 1966, Kaufman and Rosenblum 1966). In some scoring systems, coded items, social and non-social, include up to 200 discrete units. An observer must therefore be trained to use these methods. Reliability is usually measured by correlation coefficients between pupil and an experienced tester (Hansen 1966).

In addition, many studies have employed standardized tests of learning and performance to assess the effects of conditions of rearing (reviewed by Schrier et al. 1965, Rosenblum 1970, Schrier and Stollnitz 1971). An especially important technique has utilized the Wisconsin General Test Apparatus to study discrimination learning by monkeys and apes after early deprivation (Harlow 1949).

Infancy is here defined as the first postnatal year, despite the great individual variation in rates of development. This end point is also arbitrary because no clear behavioral events are uniquely correlated with twelve full months of behavioral development. Under natural conditions, macaques may remain in close contact with their mothers for more than one year, although nursing often ceases by six to nine months, and infants well under one year may be almost completely independent.

Adulthood, that is, reproductive maturity, is reached by the females of most macaque species at the middle or end of the third year and by males at the beginning or middle of the fourth year, but incomplete sexual behavior is seen even in very young infants. Maximum growth is not attained by many macaque species until the seventh or eighth year.

Early Experience and Social Preference

For some investigators, 'early' experience begins at, or shortly after, birth (e.g., Harlow and Harlow 1966). For others, it begins after weaning or some later developmental event (e.g. Fuller 1967). Research on imprinting [discussed by Bateson in Chapter 1 of this volume] suggests that experiences a few hours after hatching or birth can be important for later social behavior, while studies of laboratory mammals suggest that experiences during the first days of life can affect later 'emotionality' and learning performance (Sluckin 1965, Denenberg 1967). The experiments summarized in this section concern responses of newborn primates, and question whether experiences of primates very early in life can influence later behavior.

A study by Sackett et al. (1970) measured preferences shown by rhesus monkeys for their own over other macaque species. Three types of feral adult females served as stimuli (Fig. 4a): a rhesus (M. mulatta), a pigtail (M. nemestrina), and a stumptail (M. speciosa). The subjects were partial isolates aged between one month and six years. All subjects under ten months of age had been separated from their mothers at birth, and had neither seen nor heard monkeys other than agemates. Subjects aged over nine months had received extensive social experience with rhesus agemates. A control group of adult feral monkeys was also tested. The duration of responding toward each type of stimulus monkey is shown in Figure 4b.

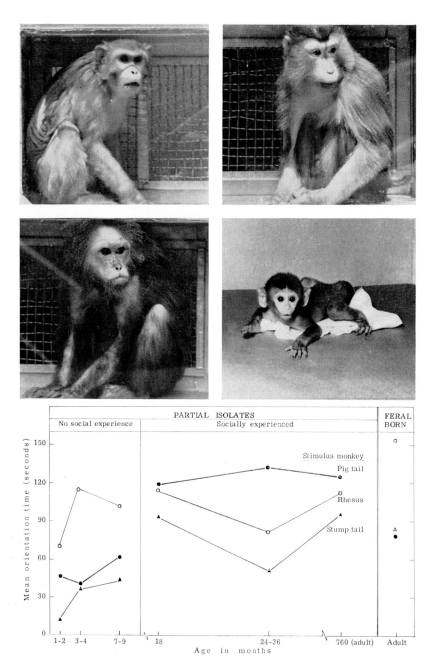

Fig. 4a. (*Top four pictures*). Adult females used to test preference by partial isolates and feral adult controls for their own versus other macaque species. *Upper left:* rhesus. *Upper right:* pigtail. *Lower left:* stump tail. *Lower right:* newborn rhesus infant.
Fig. 4b. (*lower picture*). Time spent orienting toward each type of female. Partial isolates under eighteen months of age had no previous experience with adults of any monkey species; animals over nine months of age had playroom, dual cage, and gang-living social experience with other rhesus monkeys.

Rhesus monkeys under ten months of age, who had experienced only other infant conspecifics, spent more time near the rhesus female than the others. Older subjects either preferred the pigtail or showed no preference. Feral adults did prefer the rhesus female.

The appearance of infant rhesus monkeys is quite different from that of any of the three types of stimulus females. It seems unlikely that rhesus neonates, separated from their mothers at birth and with experience only of other infants, could learn cues from each other enabling them to discriminate a rhesus female from the others. Evidently, the appearance or vocalization or other responses of adult rhesus females elicit approach by young rhesus monkeys in the absence of any specific previous learning. Such maternal cues could be important in the development of social attachments.

The monkeys studied in the previous experiments were also tested with an adult female and an adult male rhesus as alternatives (Suomi et al. 1970). All sixteen monkeys under ten months old preferred the female to the male, though they had never seen an adult of their species before the initial test. Hence, even in the absence of early experience with adults, an adult female is once again preferred by neonates and infants. Older partial isolates preferred the stimulus monkey of their own sex.

A number of studies have shown that juvenile partial isolates are socially inadequate (Harlow 1965, Mitchell 1968). The fact that older partial isolates do not prefer rhesus females suggests that initial own-species preferences deteriorate when inadequately raised monkeys have the opportunity to interact with conspecifics. This could be caused by negative social responses to rhesus monkeys learned during the largely negative social interactions of partial isolates. It is also possible that social preferences must be reinforced by contact during infancy to result in a permanent preference for the monkey's own species. Partial isolates are also deficient in sexual behavior. The finding that adult partial isolates, given a free choice, do not tend strongly to approach members of the opposite sex may be a manifestation of this deficiency.

In a further experiment, we asked how early differential rearing could influence later primate behavior (Sackett et al. 1965). Subjects were given a choice between an agemate and a woman. The woman was one of the nursery personnel who care for neonates. The test groups included (i) monkeys raised in the nursery with hand feeding, and then kept in bare wire cages for the rest of their first year (early handled: no peer); (ii) monkeys that also received nursery care for the first thirty days, then lived with agemates (early handled: peer); (iii) infants raised by their mother with agemate contact during their first year (mother-peer); (iv) six-month and (v) one-year early isolates, which spent the first six or twelve months of life in a total isolation cage. When tested, all subjects were between three and a half and four and a half years of age, and had received extensive social experiences after year one.

Partial isolates preferred the human being to the monkey (Fig. 5). Peer and mother-peer subjects preferred the monkey. Both groups of total isolates spent most time in the centre area, a position maximally distant from both

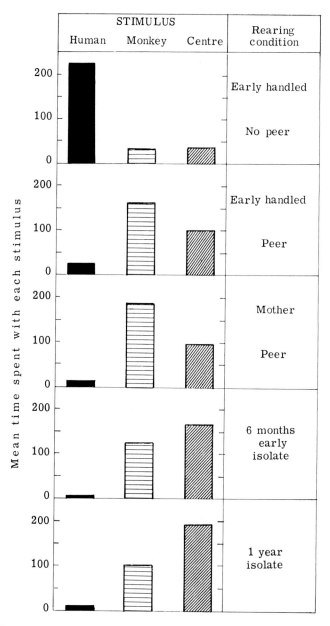

Fig. 5. Results of circus test for preference for a woman versus an agemate monkey.

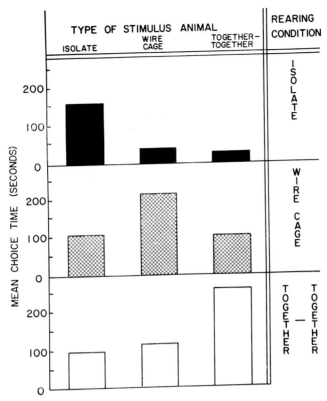

Fig. 6. Circus preferences for like-reared monkeys versus monkeys raised under other conditions.

monkey and human being. When total isolates left the centre, they approached the monkey rather than the experimenter.

These findings show that experience with a specific social stimulus during the neonatal period can influence later social preferences. However, experience of a new social stimulus immediately after the neonatal period can alter this effect. Total lack of contact with a social object during the first half or whole of infancy appears to produce a permanent decrement in the ability to form social attachments. Evidently, for the rhesus, experience during the first six months is crucial.

A study of social preferences suggests one reason why social experiences after infancy generally fail to modify deficient social behavior (Pratt and Sackett 1967). Juvenile monkeys raised for their first nine months in total isolation, in partial isolation, or with peers were given a choice between monkeys reared as they had been, or in the other two conditions. In one set of tests, the three stimulus animals were all familiar to the subject: in a second set, the stimulus animals were strangers. In these experiments like-reared monkeys preferred each other, familiar or not (Fig. 6).

Confirming evidence has been obtained with monkeys, aged seven and nine years, studied in a large pen (Sackett *et al.* 1972*b*). Each animal was scored for the amount of time spent standing within 350 mm of other subjects. Feral monkeys stood near other ferals, mother-peer monkeys spent their time next to one another, and partial isolates also clustered together. Total isolates did not spend much time near any others, but when they did so, they chose either another total isolate or a mother-peer monkey. Hence, strong social attachments exist between like-reared adults, seven to eight years after rearing.

Another experiment studied reactions to stimulation during total social isolation. The subjects were raised in enclosed cages through their first nine months (Sackett 1966). Coloured slides and motion pictures of monkeys threatening, playing, fearful, withdrawing and behaving sexually, as well as infants, mothers and infants, and monkeys doing 'nothing', were projected on to a cage wall for thirty minutes each day. Control pictures, including people, landscapes, and geometric patterns, were also projected. Behavior during presentation was recorded by an observer through a one-way window.

Two general features characterized the responses to the pictures. First, after one month, pictures of monkeys elicited more exploration and play than other pictures, and pictures of infant and of threatening monkeys produced more of all recorded reactions, except fear, than any other type of picture. Secondly, no pictures produced signs of fear until about day 80. From days 80 to 120, signs of fear, withdrawal and disturbed behavior were displayed frequently by all eight infants, whenever threats were shown, even though these pictures had not previously elicited such reactions (Fig. 7).

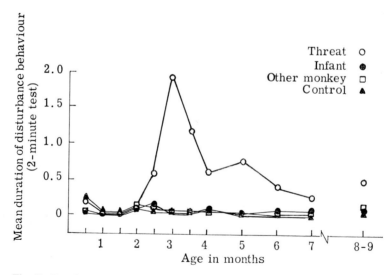

Fig. 7. Development of fear and disturbance behavior by Picture Isolates. Pictures of threat release disturbance behavior starting at eighty days, while no other pictures of monkeys or control pictures produce this type of behavior throughout the nine-month isolation period.

Fig. 8. Examples of (*right*) a self-clutching, withdrawn posture by a total-isolate infant, and (*left*) self-directed biting by a mature partial isolate.

Evidently, certain visual stimuli have a specific effect on the behavior of totally inexperienced infants. The visual components of threat displays appear to release fear, but only after a certain age has been reached [*c.f.* Bateson in this volume].

Some Further Effects of Maternal Deprivation

The production of abnormal behavior by rearing in isolation has been well documented (Harlow and Harlow 1966, Mason 1968). This behavior includes persistent stereotyped motor patterns, withdrawal and signs of excessive fear, injurious attacks on conspecifics, depressed levels of play and self-grooming, and inadequate sexual and maternal performance. Anomalous behavior persists even if the monkeys later have years of social experience with monkeys of their own age.

Some of the more persistent and dramatic anomalies (Fig. 8) were clearly shown in a longitudinal study by Cross and Harlow (1965). Behavior in the home cage of subjects aged from one to eight years was assessed under (a) unstimulating and (b) fear-provoking conditions. Isolates were generally inactive, or they engaged in long bouts of stereotyped pacing or backflipping; they displayed much self-directed behavior, including self-clutching, finger sucking, and body rocking. They also developed two extremely bizarre behavior patterns. The first was self-directed attack, which occurred most frequently during presentation of a frightening object. This behavior consisted of violent biting and hair-pulling of their own arms, legs, or body, sometimes resulting in loss of blood or actual breaking of bones. The second consisted of catatonic limb movements, in which the monkey's arm or leg floats slowly up, until it is eventually noticed by the monkey, who grabs it, jerks it down, and may violently maul it. Monkeys reared with mother and agemates never displayed these patterns; they reacted to frightening stimuli with appropriate outward attack, or with the grimaces or posturing which are among the normal social signals of this species.

Another major abnormality resulting from early isolation among non-primate mammals is a diminished response to noxious stimulation (Melzack and Scott 1957). Accordingly, Lichstein and Sackett (1971) assessed the pain responses of isolates aged six to eight years. Each monkey was given a choice between (i) tolerating two seconds of mouth shock on a drinking tube and receiving water, or (ii) going twenty-fours hours without water and so avoiding shock. The experimental subjects were raised in total isolation for six months during infancy, while controls were reared with mother and agemates.

Isolates were more reactive to very low, presumably non-painful, levels of shock than were controls; on the other hand, they tolerated more shock than controls. Controls stopped touching the electrified tube at 1.2 ma, while isolates did not stop even at the highest levels delivered (2.5 ma). Even though isolates tolerated more shock, they exhibited more generalized aversive behavior than controls when shock was not on the drinking tube. Hence isolates have a major deficit either in perceiving pain, or in learning to react appropriately to noxious stimuli.

The locus of this pain anomaly is not yet known, but a second study showed that isolate behavior is not due to preference for electric shock. Each isolate and control received a choice between drinking from an electrified tube and from a tube that was never electrified. Both preferred the latter; hence shock was aversive for both groups.

Studies by Miller *et al.* (1971) have revealed yet a further behavioral anomaly produced by isolation. These investigators studied eating and drinking by isolates and feral subjects. Initially, all the monkeys received food only once each day. The two groups did not differ in body weight. Later they were given free access to food and water for several months; during this time, the isolates ate and drank much more than the controls—up to three times as much water and fifty per cent more calories—yet gained no more weight than the controls. The groups did not differ in motor activity. These findings suggest that early isolation may produce adults with markedly atypical metabolism.

Sensitive Periods in Development

Several studies have shown that isolation from birth has more devastating effects than isolation that begins later (Rowland 1963, Clark 1968). The period between three and nine months appears to contain a critical or sensitive period for social development: animals isolated for the first three months, but then exposed to social interactions, appear to develop almost normal social behavior (Griffin and Harlow 1966). However, further work has shown that social deprivation at any time during infancy produces at least some behavioral deficiency later. We turn to these studies in the next section.

Jensen and Bobbitt (1968) observed pigtail mother-infant pairs living (i) in a bare wire cage in a quiet empty room (privation environment), or (ii) with a variety of stimuli, including toys and objects for climbing, in sight and hearing of other monkeys and people (enriched environment). Infants of the first group spent more time in contact with their mothers, and were punished by them more often; their motor development also appeared to be slower. Hinde (1971) reports that rhesus infants reared with their mothers in small cages have more of their nipple contacts rejected than infants living with their mothers in large cages. Unfortunately, detailed follow-up studies of infants raised with mothers under varied privation conditions of non-social stimulation have not been reported; hence long-term effects of these variables are not known.

Infants reared by their mothers have been studied for effects of delay in meeting agemates (Alexander 1966). Three groups of infants were reared in playpens by feral rhesus mothers. The control group received two hours of daily contact with agemates, from fifteen days throughout the remainder of the eight-month rearing period. A second group did not meet agemates until they were four months old, and a third group met agemates only after they were separated from their mothers at the ninth month. During the rearing period, mothers of the two delayed peer-contact groups punished their infants more than controls, and infants of these groups spent more time touching their mothers than controls. On the initial encounter with agemates, both delayed groups were more aggressive than the controls at equivalent ages. They had more threatening encounters and more physical attacks. At nine months, each subject was paired with a neonate. The control monkeys did not threaten the neonate, but those of both delayed groups threatened and attacked it.

At three and a half years, these monkeys were put in groups, each containing a male and a female from each experimental class (Ruppenthal *et al.* 1972a). As measured by frequency of attack during social encounters or by competitive behavior when short of water (Figs. 9a and b), the controls were most likely to be dominant. The monkeys with a delay of four months were most subordinate, and initiated threat or attack least. These relationships were maintained for one year, until all the animals were young adults. Hence depriving young rhesus monkeys of the company of agemates impairs adult social behavior in some respect, even if the mother is always present.

Similar findings have been reported by Alexander and Harlow (1965). Some subjects had surrogate mothers but no companions, some had companions of their own age but no mother, some had inadequate mothers and daily contact with agemates, and some had feral mothers and agemates as well. No reliable differences were found between any group raised with agemates. The monkeys deprived of companions of their own age were inadequate in affectionate behavior involving physical contact, in play, and in sexual behavior.

The studies summarized above suggest that motherless rearing and delayed experience of agemates may have at least some consequence for later social behavior. All these situations involve very extreme departures from natural conditions. Accordingly, a series of studies has also been made on the effects of other maternal variables.

Seay (1966) reared rhesus infants in a playpen with primiparous or multiparous mothers. Primiparous mothers differed from multiparous in the

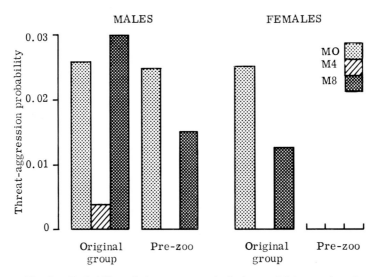

Fig. 9a. Probability of threat or attack during social interactions by mothered monkeys reared with variations in the age of initial exposure to agemates. Figures are given for the first three months when monkeys of each group were caged (Original groups), and for the last week during the six month grouping (Pre-zoo). Females showed no threat during this last week.

signals used to entice their infants to return to the living cage from the play area. The former utilized facial patterns indicating fear, while the latter used sexual presentations. Also, multiparous mothers rejected their infants more than primiparous, a finding confirmed by Mitchell and Stevens (1969). In general, however, Seay concluded that differences in the behavior of mothers and offspring appeared to be minor between these groups.

Nevertheless, studies of these offspring of experienced and inexperienced mothers at later ages have revealed persistent effects. As juveniles, offspring of primiparous feral females were intolerant of affectionate physical interaction, and failed to establish consistent dominance relations, while offspring of multiparous mothers showed little intolerance of contact, and formed a stable status system. In tests with unfamiliar adult, agemate, or neonatal monkeys, juvenile offspring of primiparous mothers played less, and were more socially intolerant and fearful, than offspring of multiparous mothers (Mitchell *et al.* 1966).

Long-term Effects of Varied Early Rearing

Studies of maternal deprivation suggest that all infant monkeys reared in isolation display at least some behavioral deficits later in life. The company of agemates, without maternal experience, seems to alleviate most of the gross deficits in juvenile behavior. Whether it also makes possible normal adult behavior has not been thoroughly tested.

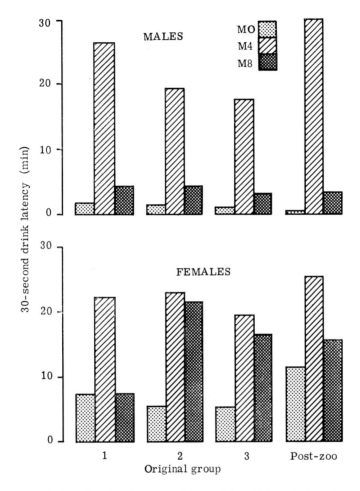

Fig. 9b. Results of water competition test in which a single water source was made available following twenty-four hours of water deprivation. Competitive dominance is measured by the time taken after the water is turned on for each monkey to gain 30 seconds of contact with the water source. Figures are given for tests conducted during the first, fourth, and sixth months after forming each six-animal group, and for a test conducted upon re-grouping after six months at a zoo. Shorter latencies on this test indicate higher levels of dominance.

Fig. 10. Examples of (*left*) an indifferent motherless mother neglecting her disturbed infant, and (*right*) a motherless mother sitting on her baby and pushing its face into the wire mesh floor.

Rhesus females reared without mothers or peers—called motherless mothers by Harlow (Arling and Harlow 1967)—are grossly inadequate as mothers to their own infants (Fig. 10). Motherless mothers generally fail to nurse their babies, have less contact with them, and reject them more often than feral mothers.

Motherless mothers have been characterized as either indifferent or abusive toward their babies. Indifferent mothers do not provide maternal care, but rarely harm their young, while abusive mothers injure their babies by violent biting or other means. Many offspring of brutal mothers die, or have to be removed from the mother. The offspring of motherless mothers nevertheless persist in attempts to cling to them, and through their persistence some eventually manage to feed and to maintain periods of contact.

Several studies have assessed the long-term consequences of being reared by an inadequate mother (Seay *et al.* 1964, Arling and Harlow 1967, Mitchell *et al.* 1967a, Sackett 1967). In general, these studies have failed to reveal important defects in social development. One major exception may be in injurious violence. Offspring of motherless mothers appear to be exceptionally violent during infancy and as juveniles. Unfortunately, the adult behavior of these monkeys has not yet been studied.

The behavior of motherless mothers with their second infant has also been observed (Ruppenthal *et al.* 1972b). Many females found inadequate with their first baby apparently behave normally with their second. Perhaps they learn maternal behavior from experience. This may be an instance of sex difference effects to be detailed later in this paper; deprived females can respond to some new experiences with positive changes in behavior.

A number of studies have described effects of single or repeated separations of macaque infants from their mothers (Jensen and Tolman 1962, Seay *et al.* 1962, Seay and Harlow 1965, Kaufman and Rosenblum 1967, Spencer-Booth and Hinde 1971). As described by Bowlby (1969) for human babies, separated rhesus infants usually progress from an immediate stage of 'protest' characterized by high vocalization and activity, into 'depression' and 'despair', characterized by decreased mobility and lack of interest in food and stimulation. Although variables such as access to the mother, or physical contact with other animals during separation, have some effect on the intensity of these effects, there is usually at least some protest or depression. Upon reunion, most mother-infant pairs immediately interact more than before separation, but a few studies (Seay *et al.* 1962, Mitchell 1970) have reported a brief 'detachment' stage of no contact between mother and infant after reunion.

Although the effects of separation are dramatic, it is still a major issue whether they are transient or have long-term consequences. Hinde and Spencer-Booth (1971) separated rhesus infants from their mothers for six days, two separate six-day periods, or for thirteen successive days. All groups showed the usual effects of separation, with severity lowest among the first group. When tested at twelve and thirty months for response to a novel situation, all separated subjects explored less than controls. Hence in this study there were some long-term consequences of separation.

A study initiated by Griffin (1966) also bears on the long-term effects of separation, as well as the effects of inconsistent mothering. Three groups of rhesus neonates were raised in playpens. Animals in the first, multiple-mothered group were separated every two weeks from their current 'mothers', and assigned to new mothers during the next two-week period. Infants in the second, separation-control group were separated from their mothers every two weeks, then reunited with them. The third, normal group comprised animals which were not separated from their mothers until the end of the rearing period at nine months. During rearing, the multiple-mothered infants displayed more signs of fear, and varied more in growth, than the other two groups. After permanent separation from the mother at nine months, tests of social behavior in the playroom revealed less contact between multiple-mothered monkeys, while the separation-control group showed most contact. No other differences were apparent. Hence inconsistent mothering and repeated separation had few effects on behavior at twelve months.

At nineteen months, these monkeys were paired in dual cages with unfamiliar adult females, agemates, or younger juveniles (Mitchell *et al.* 1967*b*). Multiple-mothered offspring were more violent than the others, while both separated groups showed more disturbance than the normal controls.

When these monkeys were three years old, they were grouped in a gang pen. Each group included a male and a female from each of the three mothering conditions (Ruppenthal *et al.* 1972*a*). Measures were taken of physical aggression and of competitive dominance, indexed by the latency to obtain thirty-seconds of water after twenty-four hours of water deprivation (Fig. 11). The

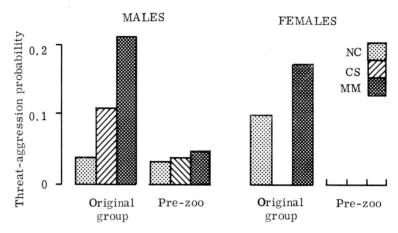

Fig. 11a. Probability of threat and physical aggression by animals who received multiple mothering, separation from own mother or normal, laboratory mothering during infancy. Social groupings involved monkeys from each rearing condition placed together in a large pen. Social interactions were recorded during the first three months (Original groups) and at the end of the sixth month (Pre-zoo) after formation of the groups.

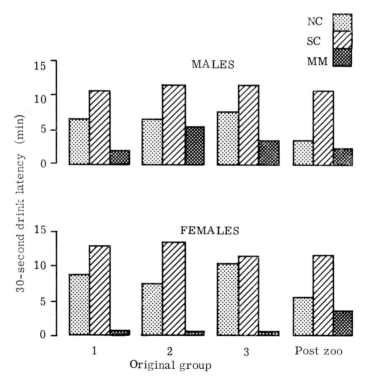

Fig. 11b. Results of water competition tests in the group pens. *See* legend, Figure 9*b*, for details of method.

multiple-mothered animals were most violent, and were dominant over the other two groups. The non-separated animals were intermediate in behavior, while the separation-controls were non-violent and low in social status. These effects were stable at three and a half years, after six months in a group setting at a zoo. Evidently, inconsistent mothering in infancy can have profound effects on social dominance later in life, and repeated separations from a single mother can have persistent detrimental effects on important dimensions of social behavior.

Factors in Social Ontogeny

The studies reviewed next represent attempts to identify specific conditions of rearing that are important for adequate social behavior later in life.

One of the groups used in these studies consisted of the total isolates described above (page 62), which were allowed to see pictures. During isolation, these four males and four females made at least some appropriate responses to pictorial stimuli. Other groups were (a) nine-month isolates treated like the picture-isolate group except that they saw no pictures; (b) nine-month partial isolates raised in wire mesh cages; and (c) non-deprived controls reared with mothers and peers, or with peers only. From months ten to fifteen, all except the last group received a battery of non-social and social tests designed to expose them gradually to increasingly novel and complex situations (Pratt 1969).

On tests of response to novelty and of exploratory behavior, the three groups of isolates did not differ in any important respect. All were moderately active, approached novel stimuli, and exhibited minimal disturbance. However, on initial exposures to a monkey partner, both total isolate groups showed the typical isolation syndrome of withdrawal, stereotyped motor responses, and almost complete absence of positive social responding. Hence the gradual pacing employed after isolation did alleviate major traumatic effects of emergence from isolation, but it did not materially reduce deficits in social behavior.

From months fifteen to twenty-six, all four groups received social experience in a playroom. The picture and total isolates were completely and equally inadequate in both social and non-social behavior throughout this period. Partial isolates were not as badly affected, but were inferior to the non-deprived subjects in several respects. These results lead to several conclusions. (i) Added visual stimulation that produces some normal responses during isolation in no way offsets later social behavior deficiencies. (ii) Gradual introduction to novel and complex stimulation is sufficient to offset some of the deficit in exploratory behavior, but does not change social behavior.

An important finding was a difference between the sexes. Female total and partial isolates were less disturbed, withdrawn, and fearful than males, and were much more exploratory (Fig. 12).

Harlow (1965) had already reported a similar finding in adults. Adult males reared in isolation from members of their own age group were sexually incompetent when paired with experienced feral females. However, some socially

71

BEHAVIOR CATEGORIES

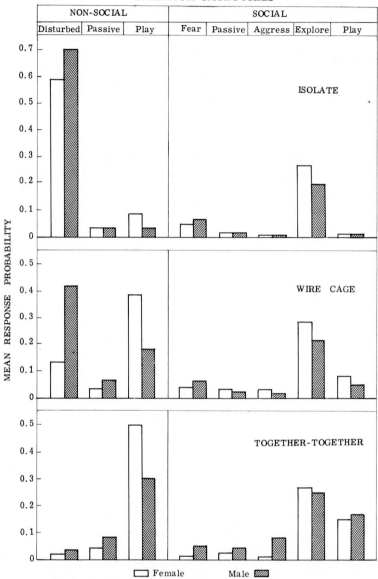

Fig. 12. Group behavior profiles showing sex differences in social and non-social behavior after rearing in isolation and partial isolation. The isolate group is composed of both nine-month total isolates and picture isolates, as their behavior did not differ. The behavior categories represent a mutually exclusive and exhaustive categorization of all responses during three months of social behavior playroom tests, conducted when the subjects were between eighteen and twenty-one months old. Differences were found between males and females in the isolate and wire-cage groups in non-social disturbance, non-social play and exploration, social fear, and social exploration. Wire-cage females also differed from males in social play. Peer-raised monkeys displayed sex differences only in non-social play and exploration, and in social aggression.

deprived females showed adequate sexual behavior on initial pairings with sexually experienced feral males, and others that were initially incompetent developed adequate sexual responses with experience.

Importance of Agemates

Chamove (1966) found little evidence of social deficiencies among monkeys raised in agemate groups without mothers. Harlow and Harlow (1965) concluded that peer contact alone is sufficient to produce normal social behavior. The study reported next assesses the effectiveness of contact with agemates in alleviating the effects of maternal deprivation (Sackett et al. 1972a).

Four rhesus infants were reared for nine months in pairs, in completely enclosed sound-attenuating chambers. Four others were raised in pairs in wire cages. Two monkeys were raised singly in partial isolation, and four were reared in total isolation. Two of the last group received non-social stimulation each day, from rear-projected pictures, taped sounds, a chain hanging from the ceiling, and a variety of novel objects. After rearing, all these monkeys lived in new wire cages for a year, during which time each was repeatedly paired with partners from each treatment group. Each pair had continuous visual access through a window separating each cage, and had daily physical interaction when the window was removed.

The behavior of total social isolates and partial isolates was characterized once again (Fig. 13). by no positive social responses, little exploration of the environment, and high levels of self-directed clutching, rocking, and stereotyped motor activities. Non-social stimulation failed to offset the isolation syndrome to any extent. Rearing with one agemate, on the other hand, completely changed the picture. Behavior then consisted principally of positive social responses and exploration; self-directed responses, stereotyped movements, and signs of fear were almost absent. Evidently, the crucial factors in social development are provided by the presence of an agemate.

This finding differs from that obtained by Mason (1968), who studied monkeys reared in isolation, either with a motionless mother-surrogate or with one that moved semi-randomly about the cage. At face value, Mason's swinging surrogate is similar to our swinging chain. Mason found that the monkeys given the extra movement stimulation displayed self-directed rocking, clutching, and stereotyped motor activities less frequently *in the isolation environment*, and that they were more likely to approach a novel stimulus. A major difference between Mason's situation and the swinging chain lies in the type of responses elicited. Mason's animals had to clutch the surrogate to prevent falling; when doing this, they could not display self-directed or stereotyped responses, and these infants spent a large portion of each day on their surrogates. The discrepancy between Mason's findings and ours may, therefore, be explained by the effects of competing responses in his situation.

Prescott (1971), on the basis of Mason's findings, has suggested that stimulation of the vestibular system by movement is critical for the normal

SOCIAL PAIRING

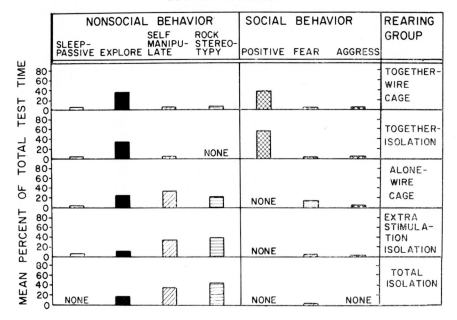

Fig. 13. Social behavior profiles comparing animals raised together in total isolation or in wire cages, and animals raised alone in partial isolation, or in total isolation with extra stimulation, or in total isolation with no added input. Figures were collected during the second year of life in repeated pairings of animals raised under all conditions.

development of Primates. Yet our isolates spent up to five hours each day on their swinging chain and exhibited the usual syndrome of isolation. This finding is not compatible with Prescott's hypothesis.

Social Therapy and Communication Deficits

Long-term deficits in social, exploratory, and sexual behavior have been the norm for juvenile and adult monkeys reared in conditions of social deprivation. Grouping animals later, whether in small cages, in large pens, or at zoos, has largely failed to induce any substantial improvement. In one study, however, aversive conditioning has induced isolates to initiate and maintain physical contact with another monkey (Sackett and Tripp 1968).

Each monkey was placed in a box with a shock grid floor. An agemate monkey was trained to sit on a small wood perch in the centre of the box (Fig. 14a). A flashing light and click signalled that shock would be turned on in ten seconds. The subject could avoid shock by initiating and maintaining contact with the other animal during the thirty-second period in which the grid was electrified. Twenty-five one-minute trials were given on each day. Isolates which had shown disinclination for contact with other monkeys over a period of years were used.

Fig. 14a. Stimulus-monkey, and total isolate showing a partial fear grimace, sitting together on the wooden perch during shock-avoidance conditioning of social contact.

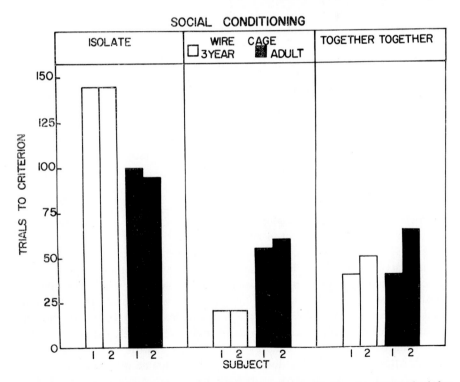

Fig. 14b. Time spent (thirty minutes in continuous contact with the stimulus-monkey) for juvenile and adult subjects in each rearing group for social contact conditioning.

All subjects reached the training criterion of thirty minutes *continuously* in contact with the other monkey within five days (Fig. 14*b*). There was, however, no transfer of training: the 'conditioned' animals, tested with agemates in small groups, were no more social than before. Several hypotheses are suggested by the findings. A likely possibility is that the training procedure was not a good one for obtaining transfer. But it is also possible that the isolate monkeys were intellectually deficient, especially in the ability to form concepts and to make discriminations. This observation matches the failure of isolates to benefit, in their behavior, from years of normal post-rearing social experiences in the laboratory.

A further hypothesis concerns the ability to respond to social signals. Two studies suggest that at least one aspect of isolate social deficiency lies in a disorder of communication. In one experiment, coloured slides of monkeys engaged in various activities were shown (Sackett 1965*a*). Pictures of threatening monkeys produced attack or signs of fear in monkeys reared among other monkeys, but isolates either explored or ignored such stimuli. Pictures of monkeys playing or engaged in sexual behavior produced exploration and some sexual responding by socially reared subjects, but evoked self- or picture-directed attack by isolates.

An ingenious study by Miller *et al.* (1967) confirmed these findings. Adult isolate and feral rhesus monkeys were trained to avoid shock. The subject sat watching another monkey on a television screen. At times, the monkey on the screen received an electric shock. This was the cue for the watching monkey to depress a lever, which allowed it to avoid shock. Thus the visual stimuli from a monkey being shocked served as a conditional stimulus for the subject to avoid pain. In different pairings, isolate subjects watched other isolates or ferals, and ferals watched other ferals or isolates. Performance was excellent when the subject was feral and the stimulus monkey on the screen was also a feral. When ferals watched isolates their performance deteriorated. Isolates did poorly regardless of what was on the screen. These findings strongly suggest that isolates are poor at receiving signals from other monkeys and are also poor senders of signals with a communicative function for conspecifics.

Responses to Novelty and Complexity

We now turn to an aspect of adaptation to the non-social environment. A series of studies has compared feral animals with mother-peer, surrogate, partial isolates, six-month early isolates, and one-year isolates, in their responses to a novel situation and to complex visual stimuli (Sackett 1972*a*). The subjects were between three and a half and five years old when tested. The apparatus used is shown in Figure 15, the findings in Figures 16*a*, *b* and *c*. In the first experiment each monkey was given daily trials over a twelve-day period. On each trial, the monkey was placed in the start cage, with the guillotine door closed. After five minutes, the door was raised, and ten minutes was allowed for exploration. On alternate days, a dark or light grey square was projected on the screen.

TWO CAGE TEST UNIT

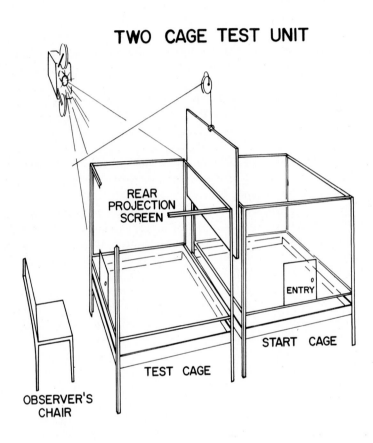

REAR
PROJECTION
SCREEN

ENTRY

START CAGE

TEST CAGE

OBSERVER'S
CHAIR

Fig. 15. Dual cage unit used to study response to a novel environment and preference for visual complexity. In the novelty experiment the observer sat opposite the projection screen; in the complexity study the observer's position was as shown.

Latency to enter the test cage when the door was opened (Fig. 16a) was a measure of the subject's willingness to expose itself to a novel environment. Feral monkeys were quickest to enter the test cage, followed closely by mother-peer subjects. Surrogates, partial isolates, and six-month isolates took much longer. Animals isolated for nine to twelve months during infancy took the longest. Males of the peer-deprived groups took much longer to enter the novel cage than did females.

Group and sex effects also appeared in time spent exploring the rear-projection screen and in locomotor activity (Figs. 16b and 16c): the groups formed an order from feral to nine-to twelve-month isolates. Feral males explored more than females, but there was no sex difference in the mother-peer group. In all peer-deprived conditions, females explored more than males.

Exploration of a novel environment is evidently influenced by rearing conditions, but the extent of the detrimental effects depends on sex. A similar finding emerged from a study of monkeys raised (i) with mothers and agemates, (ii) agemates alone, and (iii) in isolation for nine months from birth (Sackett 1972b). Males of the first two groups were more active and explored more than females. Among total isolates, the sex relation was reversed. Group (i) had shortest latencies to approach a novel object, and in this respect showed no effect of sex. The peer-only condition produced longer latencies, and the females in this group took longer to approach the novel object than males. In the total isolate group, males failed to touch the novel object, while females took only slightly longer than peer-only females to approach it.

Taken together, these observations, made one to four years after the treatments ended, reveal deprived monkeys as deficient in gross motor activity, in willingness to approach novel stimulation, and in amount of exploration. But in exploration and motor activity females are less vulnerable to the effects of isolation than are males.

The adult subjects tested in dual cages for response to novelty were also tested for response to visual stimuli of varying complexity (Sackett 1972a). Each subject was transferred directly to the test chamber. For five successive days, each of the stimuli shown at the top of Figure 17 was projected individually on to the screen for two one-minute periods. The principal effect, which appeared on all test days, is also shown in the figure.

Monkeys reared in the most complex environments spent more time exploring the most complex stimulus (small checkerboard), and the least time exploring the unpatterned black or white squares. Surrogate and partial isolates, reared in a less complex setting, explored the stimuli of intermediate complexity. Six-month early isolates preferred the simplest patterns. Nine and twelve-month isolates showed no stimulus preferences, and explored least.

A similar effect was found with moving stimuli (Sackett 1965b). Juvenile feral monkeys interacted with a movable construction in preference to motionless objects. Partial isolates used objects that moved only a little. Total isolates touched only objects that did not move, and spent, on average, only one minute in sixteen test hours doing even that.

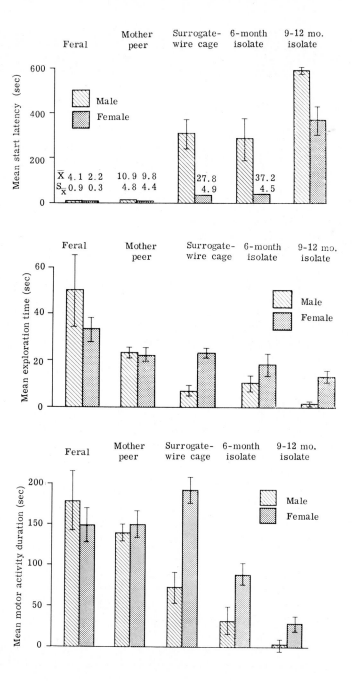

Fig. 16. Results of the novelty experiment showing effects of rearing conditions and sex for: (*a*) (*top*) latency to leave the start cage when the door was opened; (*b*) (*middle*) time spent exploring the screen from either the start or test cages; and (*c*) (*lower*) amount of time moving about rather than staying in one place. Lines show standard errors of the means.

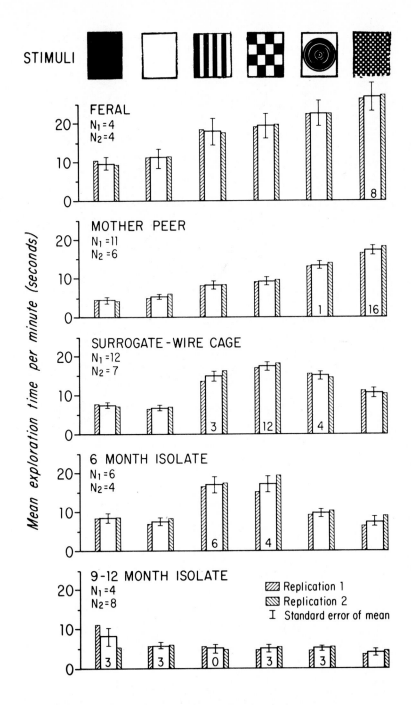

Fig. 17. The six visual stimuli used to study preference for differential complexity, and time spent exploring each stimulus by animals in each rearing condition. Figures are given separately for two independent replications conducted three years apart.

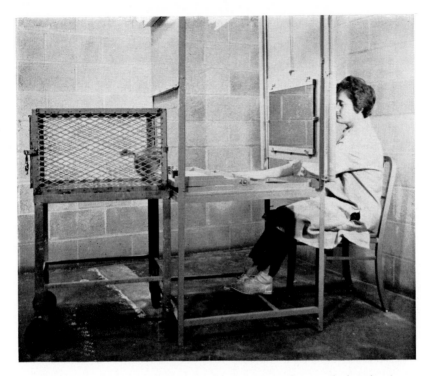

Fig. 18. The Wisconsin General Test Apparatus used to study learning by monkeys. On this test the monkey reaches through a set of bars and displaces a three-dimensional object covering a depression in a sliding tray operated by the experimenter. If the monkey displaces the correct object, it finds a piece of food in the depression. Between trials, a screen is lowered in front of the monkey, and the observer puts in the reward and the objects for the next trial. Each trial begins when the experimenter raises the screen in front of the subject. Before performing on tasks in this apparatus, the monkey must be adapted to the situation. This involves it in reaching through the bars and displacing objects on the sliding tray, and continuing to perform these responses when screens are raised and lowered at the start and end of trials.

An important question is whether deficiencies in exploratory behavior correlate with deficits in learning ability. Harlow *et al.* (1969) studied discrimination learning by early isolated monkeys of varying ages, by means of the Wisconsin General Test Apparatus (Fig. 18). The experiments tested discrimination of objects, learning set formation, delayed response, and the solution of the oddity problem.

One major deficiency exhibited by the isolates concerned the time needed to adapt to the test procedure (Fig. 19). Every animal received a preliminary training (shaping), in a series of steps, in which it was taught to reach through bars to displace an object on a tray that covered a piece of food. Controls seldom required more than two weeks before they performed the required responses. Isolates, on the other hand, took up to nine months before they responded consistently, and a few failed to achieve this in a year. This conforms with their

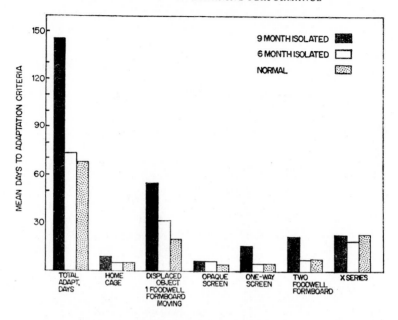

Fig. 19. Days taken by isolates and controls to reach various criteria of adaptation before learning trials can begin in the WGTA test situation.

deficient responses to novelty and complexity. However, once adapted, isolates learned as well as other animals: intellectual impairment does not seem to be produced by even the most extreme forms of early social or environmental deprivation.

Effects of Natural Habitats

The finding of persistent effects after rearing by normal, but inexperienced, mothers shows how even subtle variations in laboratory conditions can produce differences in behavior. Work by Singh (1969) suggests that findings from laboratory studies are applicable to rhesus monkeys in their 'natural' habitats. Singh captured adult rhesus monkeys in both forest and city areas of India. The animals were adapted to the laboratory, and tested for response to novelty and visual complexity, social interactions with an unfamiliar agemate, and performance on standard learning tasks. An interesting picture emerged, corresponding to some observations of human behavior and to many findings on the development of monkeys born in the laboratory. Rural monkeys explored less in a novel environment and did not prefer complex visual-auditory stimulation; on the other hand, they were less aggressive than urban animals, and took part in more positive social contacts. There were no differences in learning performance. This corresponds to the failure to find intellectual deficits in laboratory monkeys subjected to early social deprivation. Evidently, even in the 'natural' environment, stimulation during development, perhaps interacting with genetic differences, yields monkeys with distinctively different social and non-social behavior profiles.

Differences between Species

An important question is how far findings concerning *Macaca mulatta* may be applied to other Primates. Rosenblum (1972) and his co-workers have uncovered important species differences in mother-infant effects that apparently limit the generality of findings on rhesus monkeys. Pigtail (*M. nemestrina*) and bonnet (*M. radiata*) monkeys were reared in group pens with their mothers, adult childless females, and an adult male. Pigtails, like rhesus, rarely left their newborn infants, rarely shared them with other group members, and spaced themselves out during the first three months after the birth of a baby. Bonnet mothers, by contrast, kept close to other monkeys after delivery of a baby, and many members of the group were allowed to handle new infants. Infants in bonnet groups spent much more time at a distance from their mothers than did pigtails of equal age. When separated from their mothers, but left in their social group, pigtail infants showed the expected protest and depression. Bonnet infants showed little negative response to separation.

One major reason for this discrepancy concerns the behavior of other group members. Female pigtails rarely picked up and cared for a separated infant, but bonnets readily 'adopted' an infant, and tended it until the mother returned. Hence effects of separation from the mother depend in part on the social organization of the species. Observations similar to those made on bonnets have also been made on the patas monkey (*Erythrocebus*) by Seay *et al.* (1970). After separation, patas infants spend a great deal of time in interaction with agemates, and show few of the effects of separation typical of rhesus and pigtail infants. A major reason for this may be the patas style of mothering, for, as with bonnets, other group members are allowed to handle and play with the infant.

Summary

The work reviewed in this paper points to several conclusions about the development of macaques. Firstly, variations in rearing habitat in the wild, and minor variations in mothering, can produce important differences in later social and other behavior. Secondly, social deprivation, imposed in any environment, has drastic effects on the ability of a rhesus monkey to adjust to changed demands of the social and non-social environment during adolescence. Evidently, lack of social experience can impair most aspects of behavior, with the possible exception of intellectual ability. Thirdly, although the development of monkey infants may include complex, unlearned responses underlying social attachment and communication, the mere existence of unlearned processes does not ensure adequate development. Such unlearned responses, that provide a bias toward biologically appropriate behavior, must seemingly be reinforced by specific experiences during infancy. Probably most of the important behavior patterns underlying adaptability are formed during infancy; some of these reinforcing experiences may even occur during the first days of life.

Physical interaction with agemates or mothers—the affectional systems of Harlow—appear to include the environmental ingredients necessary to produce behaviorally adaptable monkeys, but the precise nature of the stimuli involved is not known. For example, tactile or vestibular stimulation, or movement of the whole body, may be important. On the other hand, it may also be that specific stimuli are not important, and that, rather, the *amount* of response-contingent feedback, with positive or negative consequences for the infant, is the crucial factor.

A critical finding concerns differences between sexes in the effects of deprivation. Females reared in deprived situations are less detrimentally affected than males. The source of this difference must be in neural, sensory, or bio-chemical differences between males and females. In most studies of human behavior, sex differences are hopelessly confounded by sex-rôle stereotypes with a cultural basis. In most studies of monkeys, however, cultural factors are eliminated. Sex differences observed under such conditions must, therefore, be rooted in physiology. One hypothesis is that lower female susceptibility results from a larger complement of unlearned adaptive mechanisms. A second hypothesis is that the unlearned mechanisms of females do not require as much reinforcement from early experience. In any case, the finding of differential vulnerability poses problems which have still to be investigated.

Acknowledgements. Preparation of this paper and some of the studies reported in it were supported by grant RR-00166 from the National Institutes of Health to the Washington Regional Primate Research Center. Other work reported in the paper was supported by National Institutes of Health grants MH-4528 to the Wisconsin Regional Primate Laboratory and RR-0167 to the Wisconsin Regional Primate Research Center.

REFERENCES

Alexander, B. K. (1966) *The Effects of Early Peer Deprivation on Juvenile Behavior of Rhesus Monkeys.* University of Wisconsin, Unpublished Doctoral Dissertation.

—— Harlow, H. F. (1965) 'Social behaviour of junvenile rhesus monkeys subjected to different rearing conditions during the first six months of life.' *Zoologische Jahrbücher, Abteilung,* 3, *Allegemeine Zoologie und Physiologie,* **71,** 489.

Altman, S. A. (1965) 'Sociobiology of rhesus monkeys. II. Stochastics of social communication.' *Journal of Theoretical Biology,* **8,** 490.

Arling, G. L., Harlow, H. F. (1967) 'Effects of social deprivation on maternal behavior of rhesus monkeys.' *Journal of Comparative and Physiological Psychology,* **64,** 371.

Bowlby, J. (1969) *Attachment and Loss, Vol.* 1. London: Hogarth Press.

Castell, R., Sackett, G. P. (1972) 'Motor behaviors of neonate rhesus monkeys: test techniques and early development.' (Submitted for publication.)

Chamove, A. S. (1966) *The Effects of Varying Infant Peer Experience on Social Behavior in the Rhesus Monkey.* University of Wisconsin, Unpublished M. A. Thesis.

Clark, D. L. (1968) *Immediate and Delayed Effects of Early, Intermediate, and Late Social Isolation in the Rhesus Monkey.* University of Wisconsin, Unpublished Doctoral Dissertation.

Cross, H. A., Harlow, H. F. (1965) 'Prolonged and progressive effects of partial isolation on the behaviour of macaque monkeys.' *Journal of Experimental Research into Personality,* **1,** 39,

Denenberg, V. H. (1967) 'Stimulation in infancy, emotional reactivity, and exploratory behavior.' *in* Glass, D. C. (Ed.) *Neurophysiology and Emotion.* New York: Rockefeller University Press, p. 161.

Fuller, J. L. (1967) 'Experiential deprivation and later behavior.' *Science*, **158**, 1645.

Griffin, G. A. (1966) *The Effects of Multiple Mothering on the Infant-Mother and Infant-Infant Affectional Systems*. University of Wisconsin, Unpublished Doctoral Dissertation.

—— Harlow, H. F. (1966) 'Effects of three months of total social isolation on social adjustment and learning in the rhesus monkey.' *Child Development*, **37**, 534.

Hansen, E. W. (1966) 'The development of maternal and infant behaviour in the rhesus monkey.' *Behaviour*, **27**, 107.

Harlow, H. F. (1949) 'The formation of learning sets.' *Psychological Review*, **56**, 51.

—— (1958) 'The nature of love.' *American Psychologist*, **13**, 673.

—— (1959) 'The development of learning in the rhesus monkey.' *American Scientist*, **47**, 459.

—— (1965) 'Sexual behavior in the rhesus monkey.' *in* Beach, F. A. (Ed.) *Sex and Behavior*. New York: Wiley. p. 234.

—— Harlow, M. K. (1965) 'The affectional systems.' *in* Schrier, A. M., Harlow, H. F., Stollnitz, F. (Eds.) *Behavior of Nonhuman Primates*. *Vol*. 1. New York: Academic Press. p. 178.

—— —— (1966) 'Learning to love.' *American Scientist*, **54**, 244.

—— Schiltz, K. A., Harlow, M. K. (1969) 'Effects of social isolation on the learning performance of rhesus monkeys.' *in Proceedings of the 2nd International Congress of Primatology*. Basel: Karger. p. 178.

Hinde, R. A. (1971) 'Development of social behavior.' *in* Schrier, A. M., Stollnitz, F. (Eds.) *Behavior of Nonhuman Primates*, *Vol*. 3. New York: Academic Press. p. 1.

—— Spencer-Booth, Y. (1971) 'Effects of brief separation from mother on rhesus monkeys.' *Science*, **173**, 111.

Jensen, G. D., Tolman, C. W. (1962) 'Mother-infant relationship in the monkey *Macaca nemestrina*: the effect of brief separation and mother-infant specificity.' *Journal of Comparative and Physiological Psychology*, **55**, 131.

—— Bobbitt, R. A. (1968) 'Implications of primate research for understanding infant development.' *Science and Psychoanalysis*, **12**, 55.

Kaufman, I. C., Rosenblum, L. A. (1966) 'A behavioral taxonomy for *M. nemestrina* and *M. radiata*: based on longitudinal observations of family groups in the laboratory.' *Primates*, **7**, 205.

—— —— (1967) 'The reaction to separation in infant monkeys: anaclitic depression and conservation-withdrawal.' *Psychosomatic Medicine*, **29**, 648.

Lichstein, L., Sackett, G. P. (1971) 'Reactions by differentially raised rhesus monkeys to noxious stimulation.' *Developmental Psychobiology*, **4**, 339.

Mason, W. A. (1968) 'Early social deprivation in the nonhuman primate: implications for human behavior.' *in* Glass, D. C. (Ed.) *Biology and Behavior: Environmental Influences*. New York: Rockefeller University Press. p. 70.

Melzack, R., Scott, T. H. (1957) 'The effect of early experience on the response to pain.' *Journal of Comparative and Physiological Psychology*, **50**, 155.

Milbrath, C. (1970) *Development of Reflexive and Perceptual Responses as a Function of Relative Enrichment and Deprivation of Input to Neonate Rhesus Monkeys*. University of Wisconsin, Unpublished Doctoral Dissertation.

Miller, R. E., Caul, W. F., Mirsky, I. A. (1967) 'Communication of affects between feral and socially isolated monkeys.' *Journal of Personality and Social Psychology*, **7**, 231.

—— —— —— (1971) 'Patterns of eating and drinking in socially-isolated rhesus monkeys.' *Physiology and Behavior*, **7**, 127.

Mitchell, G. D. (1968) 'Persistent behavior pathology in rhesus monkeys following early social isolation.' *Folia Primatologica*, **8**, 132.

—— (1970) 'Abnormal behavior in primates.' *in* Rosenblum, L. A. (Ed.) *Primate Behavior*. New York: Academic Press. Vol. 1, p. 195.

—— Stevens, C. W. (1969) 'Primiparous and multiparous monkey mothers in a mildly stressful social situation. I. First three months.' *Developmental Psychobiology*, **1**, 280.

—— Raymond, E. J., Ruppenthal, G. C., Harlow, H. F. (1966) 'Long-term effects of total social isolation upon behavior of rhesus monkeys.' *Psychological Reports*, **18**, 567.

—— Arling ,G. A., Moller, G. W. (1967a) 'Long-term effects of maternal punishment on the behavior of monkeys.' *Psychonomic Science*, **8**, 205.

—— Harlow, H. F., Griffin, G. A., Moller, G. W. (1967b) 'Repeated maternal separation in the monkey.' *Psychonomic Science*, **8**, 197.

85

Mowbray, J. B., Cadell, T. E. (1962) 'Early behavior patterns in rhesus monkeys.' *Journal of Comparative and Physiological Psychology*, **55**, 350.

Newton, G., Levine, S. (Eds.) (1968) *Early Experience and Behavior*. Springfield, Ill.: C. C. Thomas.

Pratt, C. L. (1969) *The Developmental Consequences of Variation in Early Social Stimulation*. University of Wisconsin, Unpublished Doctoral Dissertation.

—— Sackett, G. P. (1967) 'Social partner selection in rhesus monkeys as a function of peer contact during rearing.' *Science*, **155**, 1133.

Prescott, J. W. (1971) 'Early somatosensory deprivation as an ontogenetic process in the abnormal development of the brain and behavior.' *in* Goldsmith, I. E., Moor-Jankowski, J. (Eds.) *Medical Primatology, Vol.* 1, Basel: Karger. p. 1.

Rosenblum, L. A. (Ed.) (1970) *Primate Behavior: Developments in Field and Laboratory Research, Vol.* 1. New York: Academic Press.

—— (1972) 'The ontogeny of mother-infant relations in macaques.' *in* Moltz, H. (Ed.) *Ontogeny of Vertebrate Behavior*. New York: Academic Press. (In the press).

Rowland, G. L. (1963) *The Effects of Total Social Isolation upon Learning and Social Behavior in Rhesus Monkeys*. University of Wisconsin, Unpublished Doctoral Dissertation.

Ruppenthal, G. C., Dodsworth, R. O., Sackett, G. P. (1972a) 'Persistent effects of varied maternal and peer experiences in monkey infancy.' (In preparation.)

—— Arling, G. L., Harlow, H. F. (1972b) 'A ten-year perspective of motherless monkey behavior.' (In preparation.)

Sackett, G. P. (1965a) 'Response of rhesus monkeys to social stimulation by means of colored slides.' *Perceptual and Motor Skills*, **20**, 1027.

—— (1965b) 'Manipulatory behavior in monkeys reared under different levels of early stimulus variation.' *Perceptual and Motor Skills*, **20**, 985.

—— (1966) 'Monkeys reared in isolation with pictures as visual input: evidence for an innate releasing mechanism.' *Science*, **154**, 1468.

—— (1967) 'Some persistent effects of differential rearing conditions on preadult social behavior of monkeys.' *Journal of Comparative and Physiological Psychology*, **64**, 363.

—— (1968) 'The persistence of abnormal behaviour in monkeys following isolation in rearing.' *in* Porter, R. (Ed.) *Ciba Foundation Symposium on the Role of Learning in Psychotherapy*, London: Churchill. p. 3.

—— (1972a) 'Exploratory behavior of rhesus monkeys as a function of rearing experiences and sex.' *Developmental Psychobiology*, **6**. 260.

—— (1972b) 'Sex interactions with rearing experiences in the exploratory behavior of juvenile rhesus monkeys.' (In preparation.)

—— Tripp, R. 'Behaviour modification of isolate reared juvenile and adult monkeys.' Data given in: Sackett, G. P. (1968) 'The persistence of abnormal behaviour in monkeys following isolation in rearing.' *in* Porter, R. (Ed.) *Ciba Foundation Symposium on the Role of Learning in Psychotherapy*. London: Churchill. p. 3.

—— Porter, M., Holmes, H. (1965) 'Choice behavior in rhesus monkeys: effect of stimulation during the first month of life.' *Science*, **147**, 304.

—— Suomi, S. J., Grady, S. (1970) 'Preference by partial isolate monkeys varying in age from neonates to adults for own versus other species members.' Data given by Sackett, G. P. (1970) 'Development of social attachments by rhesus monkeys.' *in* Rosenblum, L. A. (Ed.) *Primate Behavior*. New York: Academic Press. Vol. 1, p. 111.

—— Tripp, R., Grady, S. (1972a) 'Effects of peer interaction and varied non-social stimulation added to isolation rearing in monkeys.' (In preparation.)

—— Westcott, J. T., Westcott, B. (1972b) 'Behavior of laboratory raised adult monkeys in the laboratory, a zoo, and in a "natural" environment.' (In preparation.)

Schrier, A. M., Stollnitz, F. (Eds.) (1971) *Behavior of Nonhuman Primates, Vols.* 3 *and* 4. New York: Academic Press.

—— Harlow, H. F., Stollnitz, F. (Eds.) (1965) *Behavior of Nonhumans Primate, Vols.* 1 *and* 2. New York: Academic Press.

Seay, B. (1966) 'Maternal behavior in primiparous and multiparous rhesus monkeys.' *Folia Primatologica*, **4**, 146.

—— Harlow, H. F. (1965) 'Maternal separation in the rhesus monkey.' *Journal of Nervous and Mental Diseases*, **140**, 434.

—— Alexander, B. K., Harlow, H. F. (1964) 'Maternal behavior of socially deprived rhesus monkeys.' *Journal of Abnormal and Social Psychology*, **69**, 345.

Seay, B., Hansen, E., Harlow, H. F. (1962) 'Mother-infant separation in monkeys.' *Journal of Child Psychology and Psychiatry*, **3**, 123.

—— Schlottman, R. S., Thorne, B. M. (1970) 'Maternal and filial behavior in monkeys.' *Developmental Psychobiology*, **3**, 66.

Singh, S. (1969) 'Urban monkeys.' *Scientific American*, **221**, (1), 108.

Sluckin, W. (1965) *Imprinting and Early Learning*. Chicago: Aldine.

Spencer-Booth, Y., Hinde, R. A. (1971) 'Effects of 6 days separation from mother on 18- to 32-week-old rhesus monkeys.' *Animal Behaviour*, **19**, 174.

Suomi, S. J., Sackett, G. P., Harlow, H. F. (1970) 'Development of sex preferences in rhesus monkeys.' *Developmental Psychobiology*, **3**, 326.

CHAPTER 5

What Can the Zoologists Tell Us About Human Development?

J. F. BERNAL and M. P. M. RICHARDS

It is unusual nowadays to find psychologists discussing the development of human behavior, and particularly early social relations, without making extended reference to studies of animal species. Indeed, one might easily be led to assume that most of the recent advances in understanding have come from the observation of chicks, monkeys or apes. In this chapter, we hope to correct what we believe to be an over-emphasis on animal work, which has led to a neglect of the specifically human attributes of our own behavior. Our approach is not anti-biological, far from it, but all too often what goes under the name of 'a biological approach' involves an invalid over-generalisation of animal findings, rather than the development of a coherent human biology.

We begin with a general discussion of the relevance of animal research, and then describe some recent research on human infancy which helps to put the animal work in perspective and promises to lead to a real advance in our knowledge of the development of our own species.

Justifications for Research on Animals

Four major justifications are provided for the relevance of animal work to research on human behavior.

(i) The first, and perhaps most general, depends on an equation of physiological and psychological levels of analysis. As many physiological and biochemical processes are common to all mammals, and maybe sometimes to all living organisms, the same is held to be the case for behavioral processes, which may more conveniently be investigated in animals—or so the argument runs. This view has become more persuasive in recent years with the discovery of the near-universality of DNA and RNA in the reproduction of living cells, and the impressive degree of conservatism in the chemical structure and biological activity of many hormones across very distantly related animals.

However, the extension of these arguments to the realm of behavior involves reductionist notions, and explanations of behavior, even if in terms of molecules, must include reference to levels other than molecular. Here the difficulties of generalising across species become outstanding, as factors such as the uniquely human attributes of consciousness and language have to be considered.

The attractiveness of explanations applicable to all species is increased by a belief, held by some psychologists, that, the more nearly their subject comes to resemble classical physics and chemistry, the better science it will be. This leads to a tendency to regard the objects of study—people and their behavior—as things that react to experimental manipulations rather than as conscious organisms that interact with the experimenter. Consequently, psychologists may be obliged to dismiss certain elements of human behavior and organisation as beyond the boundaries of their science, because they do not fit the physical model. In particular, they omit consciousness, that is, the ability to reflect on one's own behavior and that of others, and to communicate this subjectivity to others through language and other signs (Berger and Luckmann 1966). It is commonly, and perhaps rightly, believed that animals do not possess these faculties, so when psychology denies or disregards consciousness it is easy to see a continuity of animal and human behavior. But, of course, any such apparent continuity will be patently misleading if it can be achieved only at the expense of re-defining man as a complex, but machine-like, animal-object, as is done all too frequently in some traditions of psychology (see Skinner 1971, for an extreme example).

(ii) Another common justification of research on animals is the assertion that human behavior is complex, while animal behavior is simpler, and that therefore an efficient research strategy is to begin by analysis of the simpler system. But this position, in addition to the reductionist difficulty, ignores the fact that the simplicity of animal behavior is more apparent than real. Close study of animal species, for example the classic work on gulls (Tinbergen 1963), or recent field studies of Primates (DeVore 1965), always seems to reveal previously unsuspected levels of complexity.

Perhaps related to this position is the argument that psychology must be an experimental science, and that often experiments are ethically or technically possible only on animals. While this is clearly true of many experimental investigations, there is a general comment to make on the use of highly simplified and contrived ('controlled') situations, which seems to be taken as an inevitable part of the experimental method. Experiments need not involve 'controlled' situations: much may be learnt from handing a baby a toy.

(iii) The ethologists, especially, have stressed the value of work on animals for the development of techniques of observation. We certainly grant that the high standards set in animal work of careful objective observation have had beneficial effects on human observational research. However, the work of 'human ethologists' (*e.g.* Eibl-Eibesfeldt 1970, Blurton-Jones 1972) has so far been almost entirely restricted to the situations where it is easiest to regard people as animals, namely infancy and childhood; moreover, it deals only with non-verbal social behavior. Indeed, observational studies of human social behavior have been much further developed elsewhere, in the tradition of the ethno-methodologists, which owes nothing to animal studies.

A good example of this tradition is Emerson's (1970) research on doctor-patient relationships. Using evidence from direct observation of gynaecological examinations and a theoretical position derived from Berger and Luckmann (1966), she argues that the examination represents a 'precarious' social situation in which the participants must consciously strive to maintain a medical rather than sexual definition of social reality. If the doctor takes a more personal approach, perhaps believing that he ought to treat his patients as people, he will shift the definition towards the sexual. To sustain the clinical definition, he must maintain a detached and impersonal attitude, but this may leave the patient unhappy and feeling that she has been treated as an object.

Thus, although work on animals may have been important as a source of observational techniques, it is certainly not the only source. Borrowing a methodology from ethologists may have led to the use of over-simple techniques. As a further caution, we suggest that detached observation, derived from the ethological tradition, is not suitable for all problems, and that much may be learnt by techniques involving participation. This is well illustrated by Goffman's (1961) studies of mental hospitals. By living among patients and staff, Goffman was able to see the mental hospital from several points of view, and so construct a complete picture of the institution—a valuable corrective to the traditional research based only on the psychiatrist's point of view.

(iv) The most important link between animal and human research rests on the Darwinian idea of Man's animal ancestry. Man has descended from ape-like ancestors, and the study of the phylogenetic roots of our own behavior may enhance the understanding of our own situation. Of course, beyond fragmentary fossil remains (Campbell 1966), we cannot study our ancestors directly, and we must not place the responsibility for paternity on currently surviving apes, as is so often done in popular accounts of human behavior. On the other hand, knowledge of living Primates does lead to an evolutionary perspective in which we may place ourselves. It does, for example, give us an appreciation of the unusually long period of human childhood, and so lead us to expect unusual features in our development (Bruner 1972). Nevertheless, this is an essentially theoretical exercise, and must not lead us into false arguments based on direct comparisons. We cannot decide what is 'natural' for human beings, or what 'ought' to be done, on the basis of the observation of non-human Primates.

Among the valuable pay-offs from this kind of evolutionary perspective are comparative studies of mammalian infancy (Blurton-Jones 1972, 1973); these indicate that the composition of the milk, frequency of feeds and the rates of sucking are closely related to different patterns of contact between mother and offspring (and to growth rates). Given the composition of human milk, and the sucking rates of babies, these findings would lead us to expect almost continuous contact between mother and child, and very frequent feeds. This situation is found in many other Primates, and in some non-industrialised human cultures. In a study in Cambridge, where a four-hour gap between feeds is generally recommended to mothers, we found that successful breast-feeders typically had a three-hour inter-feed interval and that their babies cried rather little, while the interval was more nearly the recommended four hours for bottle feeds. Mothers who continued to follow the usual advice, and tried to give four-hourly breast-feeds, had babies who cried a great deal; very often these mothers gave up breast-feeding.

Knowledge of other species led to the suggestion that these findings could best be interpreted in terms of milk composition: breast milk contains less protein than most bottle mixtures, and is therefore probably insufficient to maintain a baby for four hours. Hence bottle feeding with protein-rich mixtures may have helped to develop a new pattern of contact between mother and offspring. Nevertheless, biological explanations cannot account for the persistence of some mothers in following the recommended four-hourly interval when this regime did not appear to satisfy their babies. For that one needs sociological analysis. We shall return to this example later, when we discuss the social context of behavior.

Beyond this kind of evolutionary perspective, we should not forget the rôle of animal work in the formation of general biological theory. (For a comprehensive introduction to human biology which discusses many of the problems raised in the first part of this chapter, see Young 1971.) To understand human development, we must understand biological development, and from modern developmental biology, which is the work of zoologists, have come two concepts—the idea of interaction, and the notion of self-correcting pathways in development (Waddington 1969)—which are central in recent psychological work on human infancy. Psychological theories which lack this kind of basis, or are inconsistent with it, are increasingly found wanting.

The Mother-infant Relations of Animals
We now comment on the part played by ethological ideas and findings in the development of various theoretical positions; in doing so, we concentrate on the mother-infant relationship in the first years. We discuss the contribution of recent research on infancy, and the concept of development growing from it; this differs in a number of important respects from the traditional behaviorist view.

Experiments on animals have been of key importance in tests of theories of secondary reinforcement. According to these theories, there are primary needs in the individual—for food, water, warmth and sex—and, by association with satisfaction of these needs, later behavior develops by a process of learning. For example, the infant begins to associate the mother with the reduction of the hunger drive, the 'primary reward' of feeding, and from this first association in the feeding situation and from his physical dependence grows his emotional dependence on the mother. 'Mother love is "cupboard" love.'

Animal studies have demonstrated many inadequacies in this interpretation, at least as a general feature of animal and human behavior. Social attachments in precocial birds [discussed by Bateson in this volume] are formed (by 'imprinting') soon after hatching, without any conventional rewards such as food, or any parental behavior that could be described as reducing drives.

The work of Harlow (Harlow 1961, Harlow and Harlow 1965) on infant rhesus monkeys provides powerful criticism of the secondary drive interpretation of behavior [*see* Sackett and Ruppenthal, in this volume]; it is also cited as support for two very different views of the importance of the early mother-infant relationship, those of Bowlby and of Kohlberg.

In his original experiments, Harlow reared two groups of monkeys on inanimate surrogate mothers, both made from wire, but one covered with terry cloth. Half the babies received milk from a bottle on the wire mother, and half from the cloth mother. Regardless of which 'mother' was providing the food, all the infants spent most of their time on the cloth mother. Later, in unfamiliar situations, the cloth mother apparently gave some reassurance and security, but the wire mother none. Harlow concluded that there was no evidence that nursing acted as a secondary reinforcement of any importance, whereas 'contact comfort' clearly did so.

Bowlby (1969) uses Harlow's analysis of the rhesus infant-mother relationship to support his account of the importance of the mother figure for normal development. Harlow describes three stages of early development. The first is a reflex clinging stage. This is followed by a stage of 'comfort and attachment', when primary satisfaction comes from both nursing and contact comfort. Harlow believes that intimate physical contact at this stage is the important variable which enables the infant to pass to a third stage, when security is derived from a specific mother figure.

The notion of secure attachment to a single mother figure, as an essential base from which later social behavior develops, is central to Bowlby's argument. His discussion, linking contributions from psychoanalytical and biological study, has generated great interest in the baby's first social relationship, and has stimulated much research. His hypothesis that an uninterrupted relationship with a single mother-figure is of vital importance for normal development has been widely accepted, and has had far-reaching influence. His use of Harlow's work is one example of the ways in which he draws on biological and ethological findings: he views the bond between mother and infant in an evolutionary context, in terms of the adaptive value to early man of the protection provided by constant proximity between mother and infant, and stresses that the fundamental element underlying attachment behavior is the tendency to seek the proximity of others. In this emphasis on the adaptive value and the proximity-maintaining aspects of the bond, he draws on the rich source of findings from behavioral studies of Primates, which have shown how the mother's and infant's behavior patterns bring about proximity, and have analysed the detailed interlocking of their two behavioral repertoires. In an equivalent way, Bowlby suggests that one can identify five 'instinctive' patterns of infant behavior that have proximity to the mother as a predictable outcome. These are following, smiling, crying, clinging and sucking.

An approach which sets the relationship between mother and infant so firmly in the context of the Primate heritage necessarily underplays the specifically human characteristics of the relationship—paradoxically so, in view of Lehrman's

(1970) definition of an ethologist as a scientist who studies species-typical behavior patterns. When this relationship is defined in terms of the maintenance of proximity, some important questions about the relationship do not get asked. For instance, what part does the early interaction between mother and infant play in the development of specifically human skills such as language and cognition? Is the mother-figure *per se* of fundamental importance, or can the important elements of the first interactions be provided by other figures? How best can we arrange child care in the absence of a biological mother?

Recent Research on Human Infancy

If we look at early social behavior in the light of some new ideas on infant and cognitive development, possible answers to these questions begin to be seen. In recent years, there has been a great increase of interest in research on infants and young children. Much of the recent research involves new techniques, both behavioral and psychological, and a new conception of infancy has emerged: emphasis is now put on the infant's highly developed perceptual organisation and sensitivity, even at birth, and on his active organising and selection of his sensory information (Figs. 1, 2 and 3).

In the field of perception, the newborn is found to have much greater powers of processing sensory information than was previously believed (Bower 1965; Fantz 1966; Eisenberg 1969, 1970). Most of the visual abilities are already functional in the neonatal period (pupillary reflex, visual pursuit, sustained fixation, tracking with co-ordinated movement of head and eyes, colour sensitivity), and there is rapid maturation of visual accommodation. It is only when we have a clear picture of the infant's sensory abilities that we can understand what dimensions of the environment are important to him. One of the greatest changes in our understanding of infancy has come with the demonstration by Fantz that infants not only can resolve and discriminate visual patterns, but that they differentially attend to them, preferring some patterns to others. Even the newborn has considerable powers of selecting what he will attend to. Much work is now being done on the aspects of the visual environment that seem to be important—complexity, movement, brightness and solidity—and the ways in which the infant comes to perceive and comprehend them. This work is very important for understanding the beginnings of social responsiveness; it suggests that the pattern of the human face as a three-dimensional irregularly-moving mobile stimulus has particular salience, and will be attended to because of its structural and behavioral characteristics.

These studies may also have clinical implications. With the increasing understanding of the complexities of neonatal behavior and its underlying physiology, it may become possible to use behavioral signs for more precise diagnosis of central nervous deficits.

Again, in the auditory field, the newborn is differentially responsive to the pitch, intensity and duration of sounds; both head and eyes are moved to locate a source of sound and to fixate upon it. The newborn is also selectively responsive to sounds with structural similarities to human speech.

93

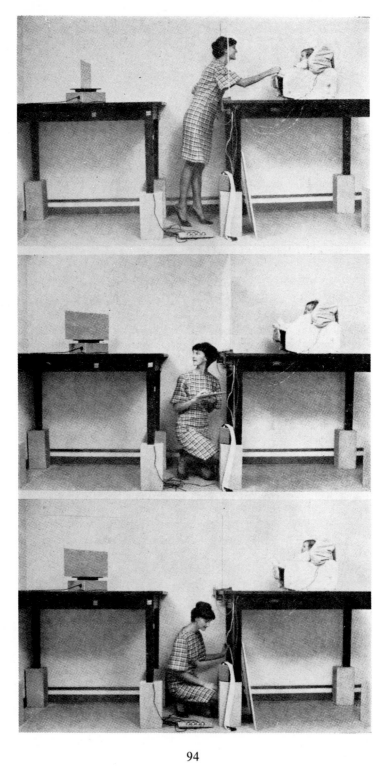

94

Facing Page

Fig. 1. Experimental procedure begins with conditioning. The infant is trained to respond to a rectangle seen in a certain orientation, and the response is reinforced by a 'peek-a-boo' (*top*). Then a screen is interposed between the infant and the stimulus area, while the experimenter changes the orientation (*centre*). With the screen removed, the experimenter watches a recorder to see whether or not the infant responds to the test stimulus (*bottom*). (*From* Bower 1966, by courtesy of Sol Mednick for Scientific American.)

This Page

Fig. 2. Response in these experiments was a head-turning motion that operated a switch in the cushions at the infant's head. At first the infants gave exaggerated responses (*top left*); later they responded more economically, keeping their eyes on the stimulus (*top right*).

Pleasure at the peek-a-boo reinforcement was manifest (*bottom left*), and was sufficient to keep infants responding up to 20 minutes between reinforcements. The problem in experiments with infants is boredom; after a while even the peek-a-boo loses its charm (*bottom right*). (*From* Bower 1966, by courtesy of Sol Mednick for Scientific American.)

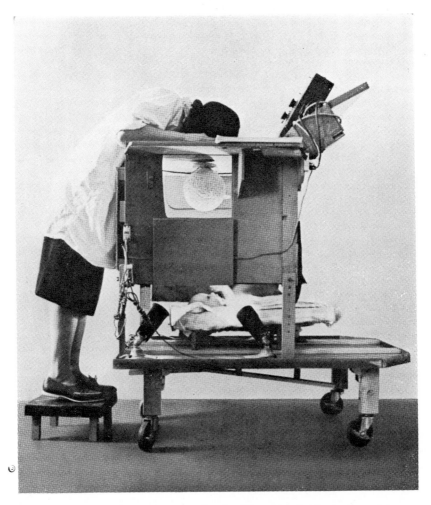

Fig. 3. 'Looking chamber' used to test the visual interests of chimpanzee and human infants. Here a human infant lies on a crib in the chamber, looking at objects hung from the ceiling. The observer, watching through a peephole, records the attention given each object. (*From* Fantz 1961, by courtesy of David Linton, for Scientific American.)

These examples illustrate the concept of self-correcting pathways in development mentioned earlier. There is evidence (Lenneberg 1967) that there is a consistency in the timing and mode of language acquisition, despite the diversity of social environments in which children are reared. Where, then, does the consistency in development come from? The selective responsiveness to human speech sounds, and other features of infant behavior, may make the *effective* linguistic environment for infants highly ordered and less variable than it appears. Thus the acquisition of language would become predictable in apparently varying environments, because of the way in which the infant structures that environment. The development of language would then follow a self-correcting pathway, since the active structuring of his environment by the infant would provide the correction. A responsiveness to human voices is obviously only one aspect of the early stages of acquiring language. These problems are discussed at length by Ryan (1973).

In the cognitive field, the 'cognitive-developmental' approach, stemming largely from Piaget's work (*e.g.* Piaget 1953, Flavell 1963, Piaget and Inhelder 1969) has provided a view of early development very different from either the behaviorist model or the maturational view of Gesell (1928). In Piaget's theory, 'schemata', central (theoretical) structures which relate the perception of stimuli with actions, are built up by the infant's motor action from an initial organisation of 'innate' reflexes, such as looking, sucking and grasping. The reflexes become adapted, by motor action, so as to be appropriate responses to different stimuli: thus, sucking a breast will be adapted to sucking a bottle, a thumb or a blanket, by a process of change and repetition of action. The different objects become 'assimilated' to the sucking schema, just as the actions become modified to suit the stimulus. The organisation of each schema is potentially enormously flexible, so that the schemata both can become adapted to a very diverse range of stimuli, and can combine with each other in a very elaborate way.

The pattern of schemata that the infant possesses at any age determines *how* he responds to the environment, and developmental change will take place as he adapts his response to situations and events that closely correspond to existing schemata, but that do not exactly match. As Schaffer (1971) puts it, 'an optional degree of discrepancy between existing cognitive skills and the external situation is required to provide the infant with the best opportunity for behavioral growth'.

This view is one that stresses the structured interaction of organism and environment, and describes a universal pattern of stages of development through which all individuals progress. The common pattern arises from similarities in the structure of all individuals interacting with features common to all environments, so providing goal-corrected pathways of development. One important aspect of this view is the rôle of the infant's response to stimulation, and his perception of the effects of his response on the progressive patterning of his cognitive organisation. As Kessen (1963) expresses it, the individual, in an active sense, constructs his environment.

There is no place in this view of development for the commonly-used antitheses of learnt against innate, or nature against nurture. All development must involve both, and given the interaction of the two, it is not possible to assign values to the importance of each factor, as is so often done in statements like 'intelligence is largely hereditary'. Some have attempted to avoid this problem, by discussing only *differences* in behavior, and relating these differences to either environmental or hereditary factors. So, for example, it is argued that differences in intelligence quotient in a population may be assigned to one or other determinant, without making any statement about the determination of intelligence itself (*e.g.* Thompson 1967). This is usually done statistically by the calculation of heritability. Though such methods are valid statistically, and may have an application in the design of selective breeding experiments, they run counter to a truly interactional developmental biology, and have yet to find a practical use in human genetics. These problems are discussed at much greater length by Hambley (1972) in relation to intelligence.

The Origins of Social Behavior

If we now turn to the beginnings of social development, we find that the new ideas about infancy can provide a fresh and illuminating insight. The infant's social behavior is placed firmly in the context of his cognitive capacity, and here parallel studies of animals can be of little direct value. Accordingly, the infant's response to social objects is considered to be based on the same fundamental processes of attention, perception, learning and recall as his general intellectual development. From his initial pre-disposition to attend to and respond to social objects, human faces and voices, he builds up, by perceptual experience, central representative schemata, first differentiating between people and things, and then recognising specific individuals. The more the early perceptual and cognitive abilities of the infant are defined, the more clearly understood the beginnings of social development become.

One example of how considering a child's social behavior in terms of his cognitive abilities can give new insight is illustrated by the following. If the concept of attachment is anchored to the measurement of proximity maintenance, there are problems in dealing with exploratory behaviour and the child's growing independence. Attempts are made to avoid these problems by differentiating between 'attachment behavior' (the child trying to remain close to his mother), and the underlying bond; this means, paradoxically, that one suggested index of secure attachment is that the child 'uses mother as a base from which to explore'. Given a situation where a child is exploring away from his mother, there are obvious ambiguities in assessing the relationship between them in these terms: is he exploring away from his mother because he is securely attached, or is he unattached?

Experimental analysis of the child's ability to recognise and recall led Schaffer (1971) to suggest that, given the child's capacity to represent his mother to himself in her absence, the internalised image could provide security and enable him to explore without anxiety.

One consequence of placing the development of social relations in a cognitive context is that one may need to re-interpret the origins of some pathologies of social behavior in early childhood. Instead of seeing these simply as 'emotional' deficits, one may be led to search for a cognitive deficiency which might prevent the child from developing appropriate social behavior. For example, if an infant lacked the usual differential sensitivity to human speech sounds, perhaps through damage to his nervous system, language acquisition might be delayed. Such delays could have effects reverberating through all the child's dealings with others, and could influence attitudes and behavior towards him. As yet, there is no evidence for this sort of effect but, because of a tendency to label many pathologies as simply 'emotional', the search for evidence has hardly begun.

Great stress is now coming to be laid on the development of features of sharing and identification with others. Kohlberg (1969), who draws, in his theoretical discussion, from Piaget, Mead and Baldwin, writes:

A social attachment or bond is conceived of as a relationship of sharing, communication and cooperation (or reciprocity) between selves recognising each other as selves. In contrast, all popular child psychological theories have denied that experience of, or desire for, sharing and communication between selves are the primary components of a human social bond.

He considers that the aspects of contact and security emphasised in the attachment concept are unimportant in the generation of social behavior, for they do not involve reciprocal behavior or a motive to share. This brings us again to Harlow's rearing experiments, this time as support for a different theoretical position. Harlow and Harlow (1965) looked at the effects of three rearing conditions for the infant rhesus: in isolation, with mother alone, and in groups of peers without mother. They concluded that 'the failure of infants to form effective infant-infant affectional relations delays or destroys adequate adult heterosexual relations.' That is, not only the wire mother, but also the cloth mother, which does provide some contact comfort and physical security, is inadequate for the development of normal social behavior.

Kohlberg uses these studies to support the argument that playing, with its interchange, provides a formative base from which reciprocal sharing develops. He suggests that 'the sheer physical need for the presence and services of the other does not itself generate social bonds because it does not involve a motive to share between self and other, or to be guided by the response of the other.'

To the cognitive developmentalist, then, the important elements for social development do not necessitate the presence of the mother, though she may in practice effectively provide them.

This is a very different position from that of Bowlby (1969). In his argument, evidence for the importance of the presence of a single mother figure throughout development is drawn particularly from studies in which the effects on the child of being separated from the mother for varying periods were examined, and also from separation studies with monkeys (Hinde and Atkinson 1970). More recent studies of the effects of separation on children have qualified Bowlby's conclusions, for the effects of separation are nearly always confounded by the effects of stress before or after separation, or by experiences during the separation, such as placement in an institution (Tizard and Tizard 1973). The immediate distress that results from brief separation has been repeatedly confirmed, but Rutter (1971, 1972) has recently suggested that the long-term effects of separation are related more to previous family discord than to separation from the mother itself. The studies of the effects of separation on infant monkeys provide a notable analogy to the descriptions of the effects on children, in that many of the behavioral signs such as withdrawal or later tantrums are similar. This suggests that the experimental manipulation of the variables possible with monkeys could provide pointers to a direction of research with children: again, however, great caution is needed in leaping from monkey to man. As Schneirla (1946) says: 'While analogy has an important place in scientific theory, its usefulness must be considered introductory to a comparative study in which differences may well be discovered which require a re-interpretation of the similarities first noted.'

Rutter's conclusion, that family discord and tension are the key features leading to antisocial behavior, brings in the question touched on earlier of the importance of considering factors operating at the 'sociological' level. The important elements in the effects of discord on a child's interactions with his family are still quite unclear, but social pressures and tensions within and outside the family must be taken into account in reaching an understanding of this problem. Here one needs to adopt a more ecological approach, seeing the family as part of a highly complex and dynamic network of social and economic forces. For example, if a worker becomes redundant, not only may his family suffer financially, but his daily presence in the home may have profound psychological effects. Our knowledge of the influence of intra-family dynamics on the child is very small (but see Handel 1967). However, Laing's methodology provides one promising lead here (Laing 1959, Laing and Esterson 1964). By interviewing members of families together and separately, these authors were able to unravel the differing perceptions of social situations experienced by the various participants, and so construct a picture of the 'games' and power-relationships involved. This view of the family enables the 'deviant' behavior of one member to be understood as a rational response to the conflicting situations in which he may find himself.

Another illustration of the rather direct effects of features of the social context on the relationship between mother and baby is given by the study of breast-feeding mentioned earlier. The breast-fed babies generally woke and cried two to three hours after being fed, while bottle-fed babies slept longer, but the effects on the mothers of the more frequent crying varied consistently with the mothers' education and social class. All mothers, in a general way, expected normal healthy babies to sleep for four hours. But the working-class mothers attributed the crying to their own failure to provide enough milk, and gave up the attempt to breast-feed, whereas the middle-class mothers were usually prepared to alter their schedules, and responded to advice from authority in a more independent way. This led to a much higher percentage of success among the more educated mothers.

The emphasis, in the recent work on infancy, on the active part played by the infant introduces another important point of difference from the behaviorist approach. Most behaviorists who work on the 'socialisation' of the child acknowledge that there are probably 'constitutional' differences between children which affect behavior, and that assuming a unidirectional flow of influence from parent to child is an over-simplification. Nevertheless, their research is structured and based on the assumption that there are no 'constitutional' differences, and that the flow of influence is one-way. A large body of research

100

has tried to relate child-rearing practices to particular attributes of personality or intellect, with very few clear results (*e.g.* Caldwell 1964). The importance of the child's effects on the parents, and of the reciprocal aspects of the interaction, are now being stressed (Bell 1968). In the development of this approach, the evidence from animal studies of the effects of young on their caretakers has been very important. Of great interest are Ressler's (1962) elegant experiments on cross-fostered mice, which showed that the particular strain of baby mouse that the mother was given to rear influenced the way she behaved. There has since been a great deal of work with animals demonstrating the ways in which stimuli from the young affect maternal behavior (Richards 1967). [See also Barnett in this volume.] There is of course plenty of more direct evidence from work with children that the two-way nature of the interaction between the partners in the relationship must be paid more attention than simply lip-service (Thomas *et al.* 1964, Escalona 1969), but it is interesting how far the animal evidence has helped to highlight the issue. Studies with animals also have a great deal to offer methodologically. An example is the method used in Hinde's work on rhesus monkeys to separate the rôles of the partners in fluctuating interactions (Hinde and Atkinson 1970).

This stress on the two-way interaction between mother and child is discussed by Bell (1971), who puts forward 'a way of restoring [the child's] contribution to our basic view of the process of parent-child interaction.' This is one of the crucial features that must be included in research on mother and child; with it we emphasise awareness of exchange and interaction within a wider sociological context. While work on animals has been of great importance historically, the dangers of the tendency to think of human beings, particularly infants, as animals, and to ignore their specifically human attributes, must be understood. For a real understanding, it is research with people that will be most valuable.

Summary

Four major justifications for research on animals are outlined and critically discussed: that the physiological processes underlying behavior are common to men and animals; that animal behavior is simpler and more experimental manipulation is possible; that work on animals has been important in the development of observational techniques; and that knowledge of our animal ancestors gives a useful perspective for looking at people. The part played by ethological ideas and research in the study of the human mother-child relationship is discussed, in particular Harlow's experiments and Bowlby's use of these. The limitations of a zoological view of attachment are described.

Recent observations of babies have led to a new concept of infancy, with emphasis on the infant's highly developed perceptual organisation and active rôle; relevant research on perception is described.

The new ideas on infancy provide a clearer understanding of the beginnings of social development, in relation to the emergence of perceptual and cognitive abilities. Possible origins of pathological social behavior and cognitive deficits are suggested. Kohlberg's view of the development of social behavior is contrasted with Bowlby's. Separation studies of children and animals are discussed, and the importance of the social context is illustrated. The importance of the child's effects on the parents, and their reciprocal interaction, are stressed.

Acknowledgements. We would like to thank Nick Blurton-Jones for many valuable discussion of the issues raised in this chapter. Our work on mothers and infants is supported by a grant from the Nuffield Foundation.

REFERENCES

Bell, R. Q. (1968) 'A re-interpretation of the direction of effects in studies of socialization.' *Psychological Review*, **75**, 81.

—— (1971) 'Stimulus control of parent or caretaker behaviour by offspring.' *Developmental Psychology*, **4**, 63.

Berger, P. L., Luckmann, T. (1966) *The Social Construction of Reality*. Harmondsworth: Penguin.

Blurton-Jones, N. (Ed.) (1972) *Ethological Studies of Child Behaviour*. London: Cambridge University Press.

—— (1973) 'An ethologist looks at socialisation.' *in* Richards, M. P. M. (Ed.) *The Integration of a Child into a Social World*. London: Cambridge University Press. (Not yet published.)

Bower, T. G. R. (1965) 'Stimulus variables determining space perception in infants.' *Science*, **149**, 88.

—— (1966) 'The visual world of infants.' *Scientific American*, **215**, (6), 80.

Bowlby, J. (1969) *Attachment and Loss. Vol. 1. Attachment*. London: Hogarth Press. (Also: (1971) Harmondsworth: Penguin.)

Bruner, J. S. (1972) *in* Bruner, J. S., Connolly, K. (Eds.) *Ciba/C.A.S.D.S. Symposium on Competence in Infancy*. London: Academic Press. (Not yet published.)

Caldwell, B. M. (1964) 'The effects of infant care.' *in* Hoffman, M. L., Hoffman, L. W. (Eds.) *Review of Child Development Research, Vol. 1*. New York: Russell Sage Foundation.

Campbell, B. G. (1966) *Human Evolution*. Chicago: Aldine.

DeVore, I. (Ed.) (1965) *Primate Behavior: Field Studies of Monkeys and Apes*. New York: Holt, Rinehart & Winston.

Eibl-Eibesfeldt, I. (1970) *Ethology: The Biology of Behavior*. New York: Holt, Rinehart & Winston.

Eisenberg, R. B. (1969) 'Auditory behavior in the human neonate.' *International Audiology*, **7**, 34.

—— (1970) 'The organization of auditory behaviour.' *Journal of Speech and Hearing Research*, **13**, 453.

Emerson, J. (1970) 'Behavior in private places: sustaining definitions of reality in gynecological examinations.' *in* Dreitzel, H. P. (Ed.) *Recent Sociology, Vol. 00*. New York: Macmillan.

Escalona, S. K. (1969) *The Roots of Individuality*. London: Tavistock.

Fantz, R. L. (1961) 'The origin of form perception.' *Scientific American*, **204**, (5) 66.

—— (1966) 'Pattern discrimination and selective attention as determinants of perceptual development from birth.' *in* Kidd, A. H., Rivoire, J. L. (Eds.) *Perceptual Development in Children*. New York: International Universities Press.

Flavell, J. H. (1963) *The Developmental Psychology of Jean Piaget*. New York: van Nostrand.

Gesell, A. L. (1928) *Infancy and Human Growth*. London: Macmillan.

Goffman, E. (1961) *Asylums*. London: Tavistock. (Also (1968) Harmondsworth: Penguin.)

Hambley, J. (1972) 'Diversity: a developmental perspective.' *in* Richardson, K., Spears, D., Richards, M. P. M. (Eds). *Race, Culture and Intelligence*. Harmondsworth: Penguin.

Handel, G. (Ed.) (1967) *The Psychosocial Interior of the Family*. London: Allen & Unwin.

Harlow, H. F. (1961) 'The development of affectional patterns in infant monkeys.' *in* Foss, B. M. (Ed.) *Determinants of Infant Behaviour, Vol. 1*. London: Methuen

—— Harlow, M. K. (1965) 'The affectional systems.' *in* Schrier, A. M., Harlow, H. F., Stollnitz, F. (Eds.) *Behavior of Nonhuman Primates, Vol. 2*. New York: Academic Press.

Hinde, R. A., Atkinson, S. (1970) 'Assessing the roles of social partners in maintaining mutual proximity, as exemplified by mother-infant relations in rhesus monkeys.' *Animal Behaviour*, **18**, 169.

102

Kessen, W. (1963) 'Research in the psychological development of infants.' *Merrill-Palmer Quarterly*, **9**, 83.

Kohlberg, L. (1969) 'Stage and sequence: the cognitive-developmental approach to socialization.' *in* Goslin, D. A. (Ed.) *Handbook of Socialization Theory and Research*. Chicago: Rand-McNally.

Laing, R. D. (1959) *The Divided Self*. London: Tavistock. (Also: (1965) Harmondsworth: Penguin.)

—— Esterson, A. (1964) *Sanity, Madness and the Family. Vol. 1. Families of Schizophrenics*. London: Tavistock. (Also: (1971) Harmondsworth: Penguin.)

Lehrman, D. S. (1970) 'Semantic and conceptual issues in the nature-nurture problem.' *in* Aronson, L. R., Tobach, E., Lehrman, D. S., Rosenblatt, J. (Eds.) *Development and Evolution of Behavior*. New York: Freeman.

Lenneberg, E. H. (1967) *Biological Foundations of Language*. New York: Wiley.

Piaget, J. (1953) *The Origins of Intelligence in the Child*. London: Routledge & Kegan Paul.

—— Inhelder, B. (1969) *The Psychology of the Child*. London: Routledge & Kegan Paul.

Ressler, R. H. (1962) 'Parental handling in two strains of mice reared by foster parents.' *Science*, **137**, 129.

Richards, M. P. M. (1967) 'Maternal behaviour in rodents and lagomorphs.' *in* McLaren, A. (Ed.) *Advances in Reproductive Physiology*, *Vol*. 2. London: Logos Press.

Rutter, M. (1971) 'Parent-child separation: psychological effects on the children.' Mental Health Research Fund, Sir Geoffrey Vickers Lecture, February, 1971.

Rutter, M. (1972) *Maternal Deprivation*. Harmondsworth: Penguin.

Ryan, J. F. (1973) 'Early language development.' *in* Richards, M. P. M. (Ed.) *The Integration of a Child into a Social World*. London: Cambridge University Press. (Not yet published.)

Schaffer, H. R. (1971) *The Growth of Sociability*. Harmondsworth: Penguin.

Schneirla, T. C., (1946) *Quoted by* Piel, G. (1970) 'The comparative psychology of T. C. Schneirla.' *in* Aronson, L. R., Tobach, E., Lehrman, D. S., Rosenblatt, J. S. (Eds.) *Development and Evolution of Behavior*. San Francisco: Freeman.

Skinner, B. F. (1971) *Beyond Freedom and Dignity*. London: Jonathan Cape.

Thomas, A., Chess, S., Birch, H. G., Hertzig, M. E., Korn, S. (1964) *Behavioral Individuality in Early Childhood*. New York: New York University Press.

Thompson, W. R. (1967) 'Some problems in the genetic study of personality and intelligence. *in* Hirsch, J. (Ed.) *Behavior-Genetic Analysis*. New York: McGraw-Hill.

Tinbergen, N. (1963) *The Herring Gull's World*. London: Collins.

Tizard, J., Tizard, B. (1973) 'The institution as an environment for development.' *in* Richards, M. P. M. (Ed.) *The Integration of a Child into a Social World*. London: Cambridge University Press. (Not yet published.)

Waddington, C. H. (1969) 'The theory of evolution today.' *in* Koestler, A., Smythies, J. R. (Eds.) *Beyond Reductionism*. London: Hutchinson.

Young, J. Z. (1971) *An Introduction to the Study of Man*. London: O.U.P.

CHAPTER 6

Animals to Man: the Epigenetics of Behavior

S. A. BARNETT

It has taken scientists a long while to outgrow the confusion between legal inheritance and biological inheritance. When Darwin wrote the Origin of Species *the phenomena of fertilisation had not been fully elucidated. Biologists still believed that people hand on their noses to their offspring in much the same way as they hand on their bank balances. Even now there are biologists of an older generation who find the prospect of a hundred-per-cent death duty equally repugnant, whether it is applied to their bank balances or to their noses. Weismann performed a great service to biology by pointing out that the state of death claims all our accumulated anatomical earnings. Our parents do not endow us with characters. They endow us with* genes.

(Hogben 1933)

William Golding's 'Lord of the Flies' describes a group of children freed from adult control. In this work of fiction, some of the most repellent features of adult behavior are described as dominating the conduct of the group. Golding's novel of original sin represents the pessimistic myth. The obverse is the view of childhood as an age of purity and joy:

Heaven lies about us in our infancy!

The first myth conforms with a currently much propagated interpretation of Man: the human species is presented, not as *Homo sapiens* or *faber*, but as a hybrid between *H. pugnax* and *H. avarus:* a blend of violence and greed.

This version is founded on comparisons of other species with ourselves, and is sometimes advertised as the last word of Science. The method of using analogy in preaching a sermon, or to bolster an argument, has probably been used since before history. In Plato's Gorgias, Callicles argues that two wars of aggression were in accordance with natural law, namely, that the strong must rule the weak. This, he says, we can learn from the animal kingdom. Lovejoy (1960) quotes a passage from the third century philosopher, Plotinus, on the perpetual war that rages without respite among both animals and men. Singer (1917) reviews the even more extensive use of analogy by the theologians of the European middle ages—the writers who produced, among other things, the bestiaries. He describes how the mediaeval writer knew from the ancients of the existence of four elements and four humours. Then—they concluded—there must be four principal organs of the body. Similarly, there are four seasons—

104

hence there must be four ages of man. This type of argument led to a system of belief in 'the physical and physiological fours'. One author distinguished four types of fevers.

One of Singer's comments displays an unjustified optimism. He writes:

A modern scientist habitually uses analogy as . . . . a guide to experiment, but he never adduces analogy as a proof of his conclusions. In setting forth his results, indeed, he usually emphasizes his inductive proofs, and thus buries deep among the débris of his abandoned working hypotheses the memory of the analogical processes that he has used.

The current writings which show Singer to be too sanguine are all based on the assumption that human social behavior is driven by ineradicable impulsions inherited in some way from a distant ancestry: *Homo* is held to be the man he is because of a fixed heredity, determined by the action of natural selection on his ancestors. But any such statement begs the question of how he develops as an individual. The difficulties of conveying an authentic message on these questions have been enhanced by the entertainments industry. Naked apes and *Homo pugnax* are involved in confused mêlées, ineffectually refereed by editors of colour magazines and publishers of best-sellers. Witticisms bad enough for *Punch* are sold as ethology. This discredits the science of animal behavior with the critical, and misleads a large reading public.

Among the critics of the popular writers are those who advocate environmental action to promote the growth of intelligence and to ensure the development of social, rather than anti-social, behavior. The clash leads inevitably to argument on the rôles of heredity and environment in human development. This ancient debate is regularly revived by new controversies, such as the recent flare-up on the genetics of intelligence.

Meanwhile, scientific methods of studying heredity and development are being increasingly refined. Though our knowledge of population genetics is still rudimentary, it is growing quickly. More important for some purposes, the new methods clarify what may *not* be stated on the causes of human diversity. So we now have, in addition to the pessimistic and the optimistic, a third account of human development, that based on science. Accordingly, the other principal question asked here is to what extent the new knowledge improves our understanding of human ontogeny

Variation

In public polemics on man as an animal, one side, the 'evolutionists' or 'geneticists', may be accused by the other, the 'environmentalists', of disregarding human educability. The geneticists perhaps respond by contemptuous references to the illusion of human perfectability. While the 'environmentalists' emphasise the possibility of change (for the better), their opponents are occupied with a hypothetical evolutionary *moira* or unalterable fate. Some 'evolutionists' also confuse the argument by a ludicrous misrepresentation: they write as if their critics held all human behavior to be 'environmentally acquired'. To state this would be to utter not an error so much as an absurdity; and in fact today no serious student of the subject does so.

Both sides usually overlook an obvious fact: all human societies are environmentalist in practice. Children are everywhere subject to teaching, and it is universally assumed that teaching of some sort is necessary and beneficial. This is a specifically human trait which has been strangely neglected by students of behavior. We might call ourselves *Homo docens* (Barnett 1968, 1973). The assumption that it is desirable to teach implies something about human variation, and it is useful to try to state these implications in precise terms.

To do this we are obliged to surrender all simple classifications of behavior in two categories: innate or learnt, inherited or environmental, and so on. This presents real difficulties, for we lack a familiar language in which to express the alternative. We have to think of two sources of variation, the genetical and the environmental, both of which vary. The variation we see in a population of children or adults is a product of the interaction of the two. This is most easily illustrated by a structural feature. There is certainly genetical variation in (for example) stature; but, just as certainly, environmental agencies, for instance nutrition, also have an effect. Moreover, we know, or suspect, that the effect of a given change in nutrition differs with the genotype of the person concerned: people with some genotypes might benefit greatly from a changed diet, while others did so only a little. Hence, in statistical terms, there are two components of the variance in a measured feature, the genetical and the environmental; and there is also the (measurable) interaction between them.

The educated woman or man of the future will need to think in this way without effort. For us today, with our inferior equipment, another description, though over-simple, is helpful. We may not say that a *characteristic* is 'innate' or—worse—'genetically coded', for these terms merely represent an attempt to substitute a seemingly scientific expression for 'instinctive'. We may, however, properly say that a characteristic is *stable in development*. This expression points to the real difference between, say, the courtship ceremony of a species of bird, on the one hand, and the pre-marital behavior of members of a human group, on the other. The behavior formerly called instinctive or innate differs from other behavior in its ontogeny. In the stability of their development, at least in natural conditions, the social patterns mediating family structure, status systems and other aspects of the social life of each animal species resemble the structures by which different species are commonly identified. Corresponding features of human behavior are few and trivial. They do not include any of our complex social behavior.

Instinct

Much of the recent growth of ethology has arisen from detailed analysis of the social signals and behavior patterns which display a remarkable uniformity within each species studied. The odour of a bitch in heat, the grimace of a baboon, *Papio*, the bellow of a male mountain gorilla are species-characteristic. Such highly predictable 'fixed action-patterns' lend themselves to description in terms of standard signals and equally standard responses to them. The signals studied are usually sounds or postures and displays; these are easily appreciated by a human observer. More recently the study of odours has become prominent.

In human behavior, there are clear parallels in infancy: each infant has his own personality and distinctive cry, yet both crying and smiling have in certain respects a marked uniformity, unaffected by culture, throughout our species. [Other, related aspects of infant behavior are discussed by Bernal and Richards in Chapter 5 of this volume.] An interesting question is whether anything similar can be discerned in adult behavior. Eibl-Eibesfeldt and Hass (1967) and Ekman and Friesen (1969) describe how certain postures, gestures and facial expressions are common to diverse and widely separated human groups. If their thesis is correct, then the neural organisation on which these acts depend must be particularly stable in individual development. We may also guess that the behavior has a long evolutionary history, but this assumption cannot be tested.

Hypotheses on such stable motor components in the human repertoire illustrate how much we have to learn about even the simpler elements of our own behavior. They represent an additional mode for the studies of social anthropologists. But it is possible to make too much of them: they do not authorise restoration of the concept of human instincts. The notion of an instinct was a pre-scientific attempt to explain certain prominent facts: for example, that most women bear and rear children, often in the face of difficulty and at heavy cost to themselves. Hence the use of an expression such as 'maternal instinct' arose from the fact that a certain goal was attained by many people. This achievement was attributed, by philosophers of three millennia, to an internal drive or impetus—or instinct (Barnett 1963*b*). (This is not at all the same as asserting the existence of simple motor patterns common to our species; hence, 'instinctive behavior' and 'instinct' often have quite different connotations —a further source of confusion.)

The females of other species can generally care for their young without special training or practice: small mammals may efficiently perform quite complex activities, such as cleaning and licking their young, retrieving them and adopting a nursing posture, on the first occasion on which they are called upon to do so. These complex performances are almost as reliably evoked as are reflexes, such as the ejection of milk on stimulation of the nipple. Women are equipped with the same reflexes as other mammals, but not with the ability to care for their babies according to a set pattern. From this follows the diversity of child-rearing practices, both in primitive and advanced communities, and the need of a mother with her first child for help from those with more experience. [A notable by-product is described by Bernal and Richards on pages 90-91 of this volume.]

Another example with no simple name is care of the body surface. The older method would attribute this to a cleaning instinct. The elaborate, stereo-typed toilet of some species is so familiar that it has been rather little studied by rigorous methods; it does, however, develop early in life. It has no counter-part in our own behavior. Children notoriously have to be persuaded to wash; and the extent to which they do so, and the methods they employ, are culturally determined.

These examples are not among those commonly discussed in the current controversy. Usually, what is debated is human anti-social violence (Eisenberg and Dillon 1971). This may be attributed to an 'innate aggressive drive'. We hear much less often of the equally justifiable notion of an 'innate tendency for co-operation' (Barnett 1968a). The importance of co-operative behavior, especially among Primates, has been reviewed by Crook (1971). But talk of instincts, or of drives to behave agreeably or otherwise, is an obstacle to uncovering the sources of the behavior. If we wish to understand how social or anti-social behavior arises, we must concentrate our attention on ontogeny, and we must try to make our analysis in terms of what can be directly observed and even measured. These are usually such prosaic items as growth rates, milk production or the incidence of disease. This does not entail disregard of friend-ship or affection, and it does enable us to produce findings which can be used with confidence.

The importance of studying individual development is now recognised by ethologists who study other species; for understanding ourselves, the epigenetic method becomes an essential. Looked at zoologically, human social behavior is a bewildering anomaly. In man we have an immensely successful, immensely social species, without any universally recognised code of signals—except those of infancy. Writers who try to interpret human social behavior by resort to other species use observations on animals, in the manner of the theologians of the middle ages, to prop up their own, already formed, conclusions or attitudes. Mead (1971) has said:

> At present, we are bombarded by .... extrapolations from animal experiments. It seems that we can pick and choose from the entire living world to find the creature whose characteristics reflect the moral wanted at the moment.

Nevertheless, we may legitimately look for *hypotheses* suggested by other species. By an irony, the most relevant observations on animals followed, rather than preceded, corresponding findings on human development. The work of Harlow on rhesus monkeys [fully expounded by Sackett and Ruppenthal in this volume] came after the classical studies of the effects on human develop-ment of early maternal deprivation. Nevertheless, the two types of inquiry are now interacting. Hinde and Spencer-Booth (1971), in a confirmation of some of Harlow's findings, discuss how the behavior of monkeys can both reinforce conclusions from observations of children, and also suggest the forms that may be usefully taken by further work.

In many of these experiments, rhesus monkeys are deprived of the society of other monkeys during a substantial period of infancy. The result may be a severe disturbance of social behavior later, when the experimental animals are allowed to mix with members of their species. In particular, there may be displays of totally atypical violence. Hence these researches are especially relevant to the current debate on human conflict. They therefore contain a further irony. If these findings were applicable to man, their implication would be that we should look, not to our evolutionary past, but in the structure of the family, or in other features of the early social environment, for the sources of violent crime and similar disagreeable features of human behavior. It is indeed legitimate to make hypotheses on this basis. But any such hypothesis leads only to a truism: we already know that, to produce law-abiding, sociable adults, we need to regulate the upbringing of our children. The problem is to find out just what factors in the early social environment influence the development of social or anti-social behavior. In such detailed, patient, truly scientific study, comparisons between species can play a useful part.

Mother and Young

Accordingly, we now return to problems of the interaction of nature and nurture. Laboratory mammals, unlike human beings, allow us to illustrate certain principles unambiguously. The many distinct, highly inbred strains of laboratory mice and rats make possible experiments in which genetical and environmental effects can be separately analysed. Moreover, they enable us to examine some unexpected complexities in the action of the environment [as Ader also shows in Chapter 3 of this volume].

The interactions between female and young (Fig. 1) offer a number of examples; they also illustrate the intricate possibilities of maternal effects when the young first grow *in utero* and later depend on the female, during their early life, for food and other essentials. This situation leads to interactions which are obvious when pointed out, but are easily overlooked.

Table 1, based on the work of Denenberg and Whimbey (1963) on laboratory rats, gives an example of the use of cross-fostering to control for the separate effects of the uterine environment and that of the nest. There were two classes of female: one had received extra stimulation, by handling, in early life; the other had not. Each female reared a litter fostered either from a member of her own class or from a member of the other class. The behavior of these fostered young was studied, after weaning, by putting them in a strange, featureless environment (an 'open field'). The defaecation score was higher if the foster-mother had been handled in early life, regardless of the treatment of the true mother, but activity was influenced in a complex way by the experience of both the true and the foster-mother.

As a further example, females of some mouse strains spend more time than others attending to their young; is this because the females are more maternal, or because the young evoke a more persistent parental response? Both parental and filial effects can be distinguished. Again cross-fostering is used, this time

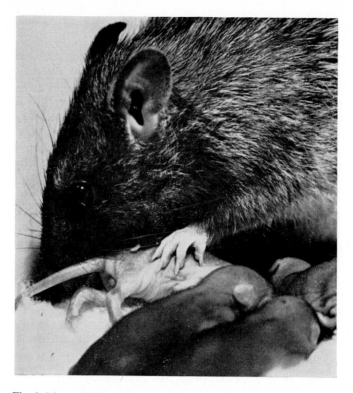

Fig. 1. Maternal behavior by a wild rat, *Rattus norvegicus*. The effect is more than merely cleansing.

TABLE I

Influence of female rat's early experience on the behavior of her offspring. Exploratory (loco-motor) behavior and faeces deposited in a strange environment. in relation to true and foster-parentage. (*After* Denenberg and Whimbey 1963.)

| | Foster-mothers | | | | | |
| | *not handled* | | | *handled* | | |
	no. of rats	*mean activity**	*mean no. of boluses*	*no. of rats*	*mean activity**	*mean no. of boluses*
True mothers *not handled*	16	47·0	6·4	16	90·6	12·3
handled	16	53·7	6·9	14	50·6	10·5

*Number of squares entered during a total of 12 minutes in an 'open field'.

between strains. If two strains are involved, females of each are observed with fostered young of each. (An example is given in Table II.) When this is done, we find that a female's performance depends, not only on her own characteristics, but also on those of her young. Performance may be measured in terms of time spent by a mother in licking and carrying infants (Ressler 1963). Hence the filial properties of the young mammal vary so as to influence the mother-infant interaction.

The importance of the characteristics of the young has also emerged in experiments in which young mice were tested for their ability to resist the effects of exposure to low temperature. Some of the mice had been exposed during infancy to moderate cold, while others had not. To distinguish between the members of litters, some were marked with a hole punched in one or both ears. In the outcome, the experimental treatments had little effect on cold resistance, but the possession of a hole in one ear conferred a substantial improvement in performance over that of intact litter mates (Fig. 2). This bizarre finding is tentatively explained by a subsequent observation: the parents paid more attention to the mice with damaged ears than to their other offspring (Barnett and Burn 1967). How parental care has this effect on young mice remains to be discovered.

A general conclusion follows. If something is done to a young mammal while it still depends on its mother, any change observed may be due either to the direct action of the treatment, or to an indirect action of the response of

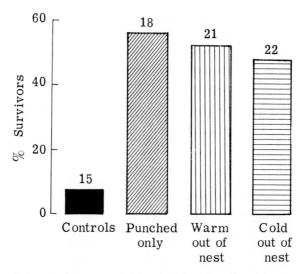

Fig. 2. Mice aged three weeks were exposed to cold for seven days. All mice had received the same handling. Controls had otherwise remained in the nest; 'punched only' had remained in the nest but had injured ears; the other two groups had injured ears and had also been exposed outside the nest during infancy. The controls, that is, those without ear damage, survived cold less well than the others. This is attributed to the controls receiving less parental attention than the others. Numbers of mice in each class above the rectangles. (Barnett and Burn 1967.)

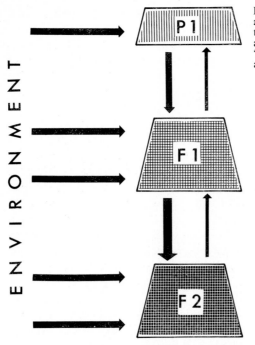

ENVIRONMENT

Fig. 3. Diagram to illustrate possible action of an environmental change on three generations. Arrows indicate how a cumulative effect could be produced. 'Feedback' from young to parents is also shown.

the parents to the treated young. The only way fully to control for the indirect type of effect is to rear young on artificial, inanimate mother-substitutes.

This is not the end of the complexities. Maternal performance not only influences the development of a female's young, but also reflects the condition in which she was herself reared. Hence we have the 'grandmother effect' (Fig. 3): the development of a young mammal may be distinguishably affected by the character of the maternal environment experienced by its mother. Ressler (1966) illustrated this by cross-fostering two strains of laboratory mice. The mice were studied in a dark box; the behavior recorded was the rate at which they pressed a switch to give them one second's light. Response rate was strongly influenced by the strain of foster-grandparents: in other words, the performance of the mice depended in part on the character of the care received by their parents in infancy. Whether these transmissions can extend unto the third and fourth generations is not yet decided. Their physiology is, indeed, quite obscure.

Moreover, it is still uncertain what features it is useful to record. A common procedure is to observe the behavior of animals when they are released for a few minutes on to an unfamiliar, flat surface (an 'open field'). In such studies the number of faecal pellets deposited is, as in the example given in Table I, often recorded. (This is said to be an index of 'emotionality'—an odd instance of anthropomorphism.) But this index gives opposite results with laboratory rats and laboratory mice. Moreover, the defecation rate does not correlate well with changes in heart rate or with exploratory activity; yet these too are

112

used as measures of the emotional state of experimental animals. Tobach and Schneirla (1967) studied the ontogeny of the response to an open field. Rats subjected to disturbance in early life responded quite differently from those kept in peace and quiet, when they were tested as adults.

To investigate the physiology of maternal effects, it will be necessary to look for a number of separate processes, each perhaps differently influenced by parental and grandparental effects. Barnett and Neil (1971) studied two features of young laboratory mice: their survival in the nest, and their growth. They bred mice in two environments, one warm and one cold. Young from both strains were fostered, some with foster-parents of their own and some with foster-parents of the other strain; these fostered young were then bred, and *their* young studied. The *growth* of this second generation depended on the nest environment in a quite straightforward way, but *survival* during the three weeks after birth depended principally on the grandparents. Table II compares figures of the infant mortality of mice newly introduced to a cold environment (immigrant) with those of a stock which had been in the cold for many generations (Eskimo). Regardless of their foster-parents, the young whose true parents were Eskimo had a much higher survival rate. This was the case even though both stocks belonged to the same highly inbred strain, and so were genetically closely similar or even identical. In this case, then, survival and growth were differently regulated by the environment: growth was particularly affected by the environment experienced by the young themselves, and survival by that in which their mothers had been reared.

Small laboratory mammals, bred in large numbers, allow elaborate experimental designs. Given adequate controls (often a difficult achievement) they can lead to findings of greater reliability than can studies of the complex relationships of larger and more expensive species. But some kinds of interaction can be observed only among higher mammals. Jensen *et al.* (1968) have observed the development of infant pigtail monkeys, *Macaca nemestrina*. The male infants were initially more dependent on their mothers, but after a few weeks they became less dependent than the females. This difference between the sexes accompanies a difference in maternal attitudes: mothers carry and 'relate to' their male infants less, and punish them more, than they do their female young. Such a correlation raises many questions about the character of the mother-

TABLE II

An example of cross-fostering between two classes of mice, both breeding in a cold environment. Mean percentage losses per pair between birth and weaning of the young of fostered parents, with standard errors (Barnett and Neil 1971).

| | | | Foster-parents | |
			Immigrant	Eskimo
True parents	Immigrant	no. of pairs	21	15
		% loss	37·2 ± 4.8	27·7 ± 5·5
	Eskimo	no. of pairs	20	19
		% loss	14·9 ± 2·3	10·8 ± 2·0

infant interaction of this and other species, and suggests some interesting experiments to test hypothesized causal relationships.

What implications have these findings for ourselves? There can be no direct application from mice or even monkeys to men, but we are justified in looking for interactions of the same general form. From the studies, still rudimentary, of other species, we can discern (i) subtle effects of the early environment and (ii) the possibilities of grandmother effects, as well as the complications of genetical differences. Moreover, the action of the environment changes with the genotype acted upon.

Cultural Transmissions

Such observations remind us of the concealed interactions which can occur in a human family. Parents do not only educate their children: they may be educated by them. Study of other species may also give us a frame of reference in which to set observations on the stability and instability of cultural patterns. It is a far cry from litters of mice to societies of men, but the formal structure of the interactions may be the same. In general, the children of emigrants to a new country with a strange culture may be expected rapidly to adopt the local way of life. This has been exemplified on a large scale in North America, and it reflects the lability of human social development, and the lack of correspondence between anatomical characteristics and behavior. Nevertheless, there are striking exceptions, for instance among the Jewish colonies of Abyssinia, South India and China. Although, therefore, social behavior can change very quickly, there have been societies in which—at least in some respects—it has been more stable than structural (the so-called 'racial') features. The analysis of the mechanisms of tradition requires an understanding of the parent-young inter-actions that determine social attitudes. It is for those working in the social sciences to decide whether the simpler relationships we record among other species provide models on which to base observations or hypotheses concerning men.

The Complexities of Habit Formation

If environmental actions are so various and subtle, we must expect to find examples in the development of the ability to adapt behavior to circumstances. Here it is useful to distinguish between training for specific skills and more general effects.

Consider what happens if a mammal is trained to find its way through a maze. This involves developing a specific habit, namely, running, swimming or otherwise moving, with the greatest economy of effort, from one point to another. Such an achievement might, *a priori*, be expected to interfere with the development of other, similar habits; but, as is well known, the opposite is true: experience of learning one maze improves later performance on others (Marx 1944). This phenomenon, learning set, is quite general, and has been much studied in Primates (Harlow 1959). It is analogous to the comprehension, by a human being, of the logical structure of a class of problems.

As an example, we have the oddity puzzle. An animal is presented with three objects, of which two are alike. To obtain a reward, it must always choose the odd object, regardless of what that object is. Rats achieve this only with the utmost difficulty, but monkeys do so easily. In solving such a problem, animals have to abstract, in each situation, a general property of the objects presented; instead of responding to particular objects (their shapes, textures or odours), they must be guided by the difference (any difference) of one object from the other two. Hence they must identify a common formal structure in a number of different situations. Yet a further example is provided by experiments in which animals are required to learn to choose one of two objects, and then to reverse their choice. When a mammal is repeatedly trained on such reversals, its performance improves steadily; not only can it learn to choose A rather than B, but it can also learn something more general, namely, *changing* its preference in either direction (Mackintosh 1969).

Another well-established phenomenon, also much studied by the use of mazes, is 'latent learning' (reviewed by Barnett 1963a). When an animal is trained in a maze, it receives, on reaching the goal, food or some other reward which matches a deficit already induced by the experimenter. If a small mammal, not fasted or otherwise deprived, is put in a maze which contains no special incentive, it nevertheless wanders about. During its explorations it unobtrusively stores information. This is shown if it is subsequently trained to run from one point to another in the maze: its performance surpasses that of a control animal with no previous experience of the situation.

The Development of Intelligence

The phenomena described above are displayed by adults. For our present purpose, effects of early experience are more important. The typical environment of a small laboratory mammal is quite abnormal: it confines the animal in a small space, and is markedly lacking in feature. A human description might include the word 'boring'. Hebb (1949) saw the importance of this, and opened a new area of inquiry into its effects. In many experiments since then, animals reared in small cages have been compared with others given a more generous early experience. By an unbiological inversion, the animals allowed a complex ('enriched') environment are often called the experimental group, those in pathogenic restriction, the controls.

All enquiries of this kind have pointed in the same direction: young mammals reared in almost featureless, unstimulating conditions are less intelligent than those given diverse experience or extra stimulation. By 'less intelligent' is meant less able to solve the problems of standard 'learning' situations in the laboratory—discriminations, problem boxes, mazes and so on. [These findings illustrate the phenomena of sensitive periods in development also discussed by Bateson and by Ader in this volume.]

An important question concerns the generality of the effects. The measurement of human abilities has led to debate on the existence of 'general intelligence'. Similarly, it may be asked whether laboratory rats can be *generally* improved

115

'intellectually' by early stimulation. In fact, as might be expected, there is no good evidence that they can. Gibson and Walk (1956) exposed rats during infancy to black triangles and circles on white cage walls; the cages of the controls were plain. Later, the experimental group learnt to discriminate circles from triangles more quickly, and with fewer errors, than the controls. This was evidently a purely sensory effect. Forgus (1955) studied the relative importance of sensory and motor experiences. One group of rats was given much early visual and motor experience in a complex environment; a second group had similar visual experience, but little opportunity to move about. As adults, the second group did better in a test of maze learning if the lights were on, but the first group did better in darkness, that is, in conditions in which movement had to be based on kinaesthesia. Such findings suggest that early training confers some degree of problem-solving ability, but that each aspect of the training influences performance only in those problems which involve the use of particular motor or sensory systems.

Experiments with enriched or impoverished environments alter the inputs through all the external senses. Important studies have also been made on animals deprived of the visual stimulation usually received in early life, but otherwise raised in a normal environment; others have been made of animals prevented from receiving the proprioceptive input normally associated with movement (Held and Hein 1963). A kitten quite early develops the ability to make accurate movements of the limbs in relation to objects or surfaces. At first we might suppose this to be an affair of maturation, independent of experience. But if a kitten is deprived of the sight of its limbs by a large plastic collar, it fails to develop the normal, accurate placing response of the forelimbs, even though there is otherwise unrestricted visual experience and freedom to move about. Other experiments have shown how normal responses to visual stimuli develop only if the animal experiences the proprioceptive input from walking or running.

Primates, too, have been studied. Held and Bauer (1967) reared macaques from birth in conditions in which they could not see their bodies. When allowed to see one hand at thirty-five days they were unable to guide it visually. Fortunately, by four months, the abilities of the experimental animals had swung back on to the normal curve of development displayed by the controls.

The implications of these findings, both for normal development and for the training of spastic children, have been reviewed by Connolly (1969). A crucial question concerns the extent to which the conclusions of carefully designed experiments on other species may be applied to man. Ethically acceptable experiments are rarely possible on human beings, but some observations by White and Held (1967) make an exception. They studied babies under care in an institution. During the second to fifth weeks of life the infants were given extra stimulation daily by handling them for twenty minutes. This led to an increase in visual exploration and visually guided reaching. These authors also gave some infants extra visual stimulation only, and so provoked visual exploration, but reduced movements of the arms.

116

A beginning has been made on the neurology of early visual experience, based partly on studies of people with errors of refraction not corrected in early life and partly on experiments on kittens reared in visually deficient environments (Shlaer 1971, Freeman *et al.* 1972). Astigmatism can, according to Freeman and his colleagues, leave a lasting central nervous deficit of acuity in the perception of vertical or horizontal lines, corresponding to the character of the astigmatism. Kittens with an experimentally induced squint evidently develop an abnormal relationship between the left and right visual areas of the cerebral cortex. These observations, if confirmed, reveal a new dimension of the interaction between nature and nurture: evidently, at a very early age, the establishment of normal brain function requires quite specific stimulation; or this depends the perception of primary properties of the environment.

Learning Processes

There are other implications, from work on animals, for the intellectual development of normal children. From the vast mass of researches on 'learning', two items may be taken as having such implications: (i) storage of information by contiguity, that is, independently of reward or response, and (ii) the effects of punishment.

The first principle conflicts with recent conventional teaching. For much of this century, textbooks of physiology have unthinkingly included a brief account of Pavlov's studies of conditional reflexes. There has often been no attempt to describe the actual complexities of central nervous functioning in the control of behavior, still less the problems that remain to be solved. Unfortunate students have been given an impression of brain function and behavior which corresponds to the way in which some electrical machines work, but has no useful connexion with what the mammalian central nervous system does.

Pavlov's technique can be used for the study of autonomic responses, including the eye-blink, and for tendon reflexes. Even then, the findings from such work reflect the formidable intricacies of the mammalian brain (Razran 1971): they do not lend themselves to any simple, electronic interpretations.

In the very different, but still highly contrived, situations associated with the names of Thorndike and Skinner, the development of simple habits is typically regulated by the character of the reward offered. Both Thorndike's and Skinner's methods have made their contribution. What we can now see, and must emphasise, is how much they omit. In Skinner's system, 'learning', in all its complexity of registration, information storage and information retrieval (Bovet *et al.* 1968), has been represented as simply a matter of schedules of reward and punishment. Yet the phenomena of latent learning, learning set, and early learning to learn (discussed above on pages 114-116) all illustrate how much information may be stored as a result simply of exposure to stimulation. Much of the multiplex assembly of processes we discuss under the rubric of 'learning' takes place without reward or punishment or, indeed, any obvious incentive. Only contiguity is needed.

117

'Schedules of reinforcement' certainly do not account for the information stored during incidental stimulation. Similarly, naive interpretations of the effects of punishment do not correspond to the facts. In experimental studies, 'punishment' means stimulation that tends to cause avoidance, and is a consequence of some act by the experimental subject. The punishment most commonly used in the laboratory, namely, an electric shock to the feet, is very unlike anything that happens in natural conditions. If the shock is severe, a single experience may make an animal avoid the whole situation in which it has occurred (Church 1969). It is this kind of observation, no doubt, which has led some psychologists to state that punishment of human beings (among whom children should be included!) is a completely ineffective method of teaching skills. This may be regarded as a hypothesis, based on an analogy with animal behavior, that should be tested more thoroughly.

In laboratory experiments it is more usual to use very mild shocks. Sometimes these have the effect predicted by common sense: the animal is deterred from performing the act which led to the shock. But, if an animal is simultaneously both rewarded and punished, for example by receiving both a mild shock and food at the same time, the habit which led to this occurrence may be encouraged: sometimes, in fact, a stimulus which is usually aversive *strengthens* the habit that leads to it (Fowler and Wischner 1969). Such observations may lead us to reflect on the use of punishment in human communities. There seems to be rather little exact information on its effects on the training of children. Aronson and Carlsmith (1963) threatened children either with severe punishment or with mild punishment for playing with certain toys. The mild threat had the greater effect. So many variables enter into these situations, it is hardly possible to attempt valid generalisations without much more information, but what is known warns us against hasty assumptions.

Attitudes to punishment, like those to race or the genetics of intelligence, are likely to be greatly influenced by personal bias. Punishment also provides a notable opportunity for argument by analogy. In the social behavior of other species, punishment is employed only in relation to spacing individuals out: it occurs (i) when young are weaned by their mother, (ii) when a status system (or dominance hierarchy) entails separation of individuals of different standing, and (iii) in the defence of territory. If one dislikes punishment, and is willing to use a valueless argument, one may point to the animals and say how wrong we are to try to teach our children skills by punishing them. On the other hand, it is equally valid to say that human beings are so adaptable that even pain can be used to induce them to develop new and useful habits. Of course, what we need is exact information about what actually happens.

Play

Theories of learning in terms of conditioning, Pavlovian or operant, are attractive because they make complex and baffling phenomena seem comprehensible. Experiments on punishment show how misleading it is to imply that its effects are simple. Much behavior, especially in natural conditions, is so disorderly that it defies even precise description, An example is play. We give this name to a variety of familiar activities. Loizos (1966) lists features characteristic of these activities. They are commonly fragmented, and irrelevant to the situation in which they are performed; they are repetitive; and they are often exaggerated and made up of components performed out of their normal, adult sequence. Despite all this, there are many occasions when behavior would be identified as play by any observer.

It is usually assumed that play allows the player to practice what will later be performed in earnest. Certainly, there are as many types of play as there are of complex behavior. Predatory mammals perform, at least in early life, activities which resemble hunting. Young mammals threaten each other, mount each other in a sexual manner, and run about erratically. Juvenile females of some species of Primates even indulge in 'play-mothering' (Lancaster 1971).

One reason why play has baffled workers on behavior is its heterogeneity. If all the activities called 'play' have some practice function, then it should be possible to interpret them in terms of information storage. We have seen how, especially in early life, lasting changes in brain function result from the type of stimulation experienced. Perhaps play has as many effects on the development of the brain as there are types of memory. If so, it is not surprising that it takes many forms.

Conclusions

Any attempt to relate experiments on animals to problems of human development reveals how little is known on matters of crucial importance to every parent, teacher or clinician. But, as the whole of this volume shows, methods now exist which can give us exact knowledge in fields in which hitherto folk-lore has often been a more reliable guide than science. To apply these methods fully, the collaboration of people from diverse disciplines is needed. Many instances are given in a previous volume of this series (Wolff and Mac Keith 1969).

There is still great scope for detailed analysis of the behavior of mothers and children. Bernal and Richards [in this volume] give an example in which, for a fruitful hypothesis about behavior, knowledge of the chemistry of the milk of different species was necessary.

A major area of research, up to now for the most part studied only piecemeal, includes the phenomena of exploratory behavior and play, and also the effects of stimulation or lack of it on the development of the brain and of all aspects of behavior. A crucial question, still unanswered, concerns the *lasting* effects of different kinds and levels of stimulation in infancy. Experiments on animals suggest (by analogy) that we cannot afford to leave infants or young children in boring surroundings, but no precise statements are yet possible on the effects of exactly defined conditions of upbringing on measurable features of development. There is, however, good evidence that the development of children with defects of sensori-motor function may be impaired by the secondary consequences of their condition, unless compensation is made for the diminished input to the central nervous system; if this is not done, intellectual development may be retarded (Abercrombie 1968).

It is coming to be realised that a mother not only provides milk and other obvious necessities, but is also a continual source of stimulation, by contact, sound and sight. For some species of mammals, tactile stimulation by the mother (or some experimental substitute) is essential if the neonate is to develop the normal reflexes of elimination. No needs of such precise specificity have been detected in our own species, but we may suspect that what Shaw called 'maternal massage' is continually having concealed effects of great subtlety and importance. The well established effect of early stimulation on the development of the intelligence of laboratory mammals is evidently only one aspect of a fundamental phenomenon: the central nervous system of a mammal, and still more of a man, is so plastic that—especially in early life—it is continually storing information and modifying its mode of operation as a result of the input it receives.

Infancy is not only a period of establishing sensory and sensori-motor function. An infant in the first year may no longer be regarded as a 'sense-dominated automaton'. Even at the age of nine months, as ingenious experiments have shown, thought—in the sense of hypothesis-formation—evidently begins (Kagan 1971). (This conflicts with the widely propagated views of Piaget.)

An urgent task for the immediate future is to enlarge on the pioneering work of those who have begun research in this difficult field; this will require lengthy projects, in which behavioral and neural changes receive very detailed analysis. Experiments on laboratory animals (especially Primates) and observations of children by psychologists and clinicians should be linked with comparative studies of diverse communities and different social groups within communities. The effects of varying conditions of rearing which need to be studied include not only the growth of intelligence and of social behavior, but also the incidence of mental illness and even of resistance to organic disease.

Such projects should be founded on an authentic human biology. The Western literary sub-culture is at present obsessed with gloomy accounts of the human predicament, or of the Awfulness of Man, but this attitude has no valid basis in what we know of human or animal behavior. *Homo* may not always be as *sapiens* as we wish, but he is certainly adaptable, in two senses.

The first kind of adaptibility he shares with organisms in general: over many generations human populations can change genetically, in response to the demands of the environment. This is the natural-selection process; it results from the superior fertility or longevity of some genetical types compared with others. It is a slow process in relation to a human lifetime, but on the geological time-scale it can be rapid (Ford 1964). Something is known of such changes in our resistance to disease, but on behavior all is surmise. Nevertheless, we know enough to reject certain assumptions made by popular writers on human evolution. According to them, our ancestors of a few million years ago displayed certain firmly fixed behavioral propensities, and *therefore* we do so too. The first part of such an assertion cannot be tested; but, in any case, the second part is a *non sequitur*, for it disregards the possibilities offered by genetical variation. There is no reason to suppose the human genotype to have stuck even in the quite recent hunter-gatherer stage. Perhaps there has been selection for adaptability of behavior, as a result of the development of tool-making. This speculation does not lead to any programme by which it could be verified, but it warns us against descriptions of man in terms of predetermined or 'pre-programmed' components of behavior.

The second sense in which man is highly adaptable is reflected in his having no one natural habitat or mode of existence: we are not specifically adapted to life in grassy plains, like baboons, or in tropical forest, like gorillas; human beings live in both these environments and many others as well. This parallels our lack of universal, species-characteristic forms of behavior.

Despite the lability of our behavior, some human communities, savage or peasant, have remained stable for tens of generations. This is not a consequence of genetical uniformity: there is no one human genotype; man is highly poly-morphic. Even a small community commonly displays great genetical hetero-geneity. There is also always some component of cultural instability. Human social organisation not only allows continuity, but also confers the 'capacity for transcending what is learned; a potentiality for innovation, creativity, reorganisation and change' (Hallowell 1960).

The stable forms of human social organisation are many; stability depends, not on gestures and sounds common to our whole species, but on social relation-ships of a higher generality. In all human communities, stable or changing, social (and other) behavior is a product of the teaching of young by their elders; that is, it depends on tradition. This exceedingly complex sort of behavior, notably under-researched, is special to man (Barnett 1968, 1973). Questions on the biological nature of man have therefore been wrongly stated. We lack standard social signals and social forms, yet we succeed in maintaining societies of steadily increasing size and complexity. How is this achieved? The ability to store information at all times and, more significant still, to imitate and to teach, are foundations of all human societies. On them depends the realisation of our capacities for intelligent or stupid behavior, and for co-operation or conflict. The ground for hope for the future lies in our ability to control our own learning and teaching.

Summary
The study of individual development, from before birth to maturity, is the key to understanding human intelligence and social behavior. All behavior is influenced by both the genotype and the environment, but some features of behavior develop more reliably, that is, are less affected by environmental variation, than others. The social behavior patterns of animals are uniform for each species, usually stable in development, and are each related to a single ecological niche; they have been called 'innate' (an inappropriate term) or 'instinctive' (ambiguous). Human social behavior, by contrast, is adapted to

121

no single mode of life or habitat, and does not depend on a code of universally recognised signals.

The current use of analogies with other species as proof of propositions about human behavior represents a regression to pre-scientific modes of thought. Nevertheless, despite the differences from man, studies of other species, such as the experimental analyses of mother-young relationships described in this chapter, can provide hypotheses (which must be tested) about human behavior, and still more about human physiology. They may also provide models of types of interaction.

The plasticity of human behavior depends on the ability of the brain continuously to store information, and to modify its functioning with experience. This takes place independently of reward or punishment. Studies of the early post-natal life of both man and other mammals have recently revealed environmental effects of previously unsuspected subtlety and importance.

In the absence of species-characteristic ('instinctive') social patterns, human social and intellectual development depends on the particular environment provided by the family or community: all human beings have some propensity for both intelligent and stupid behavior, for both pacificism and violence, and for both philoprogenitiveness and misanthropy. Despite the genetical heterogeneity present in every human population, the extent to which these propensities are realised largely depends on the character of the early environment. In every human community the young not only imitate their elders but are taught by them. Teaching, a distinctive feature of our species, is conservative yet allows continual social change.

Modern research methods promise a rapid advance in our knowledge of human development. The methods should be applied in a framework of an authentic human biology, by workers drawn from diverse fields.

REFERENCES

Abercrombie, M. L. J. (1968) 'Some notes on spatial disability: movement, intelligence quotient and attentiveness.' *Developmental Medicine and Child Neurology*, **10**, 206.

Aronson, E., Carlsmith, J. M. (1963) 'Effect of the severity of threat on the devaluation of forbidden behavior.' *Journal of Abnormal and Social Psychology*, **66**, 585.

Barnett, S. A. (1963a) *A Study in Behaviour*. London: Methuen.

—— (1963b) 'Instinct.' *Daedalus*, **92**, 564.

—— (1968) 'The "instinct to teach".' *Nature (London)*, **220**, 747.

—— (1971) *The Human Species*, 5th edn. London: MacGibbon & Kee.

—— (1973) 'Homo docens.' *Journal of Biosocial Science*. (In the press.)

—— Burn, J. (1967) 'Early stimulation and maternal behaviour.' *Nature (London)*, **213**, 150.

—— Neil, A. C. (1971) 'Growth and reproduction of mice cross-fostered between parents reared at different temperatures.' *Journal of Physiology*, **215**, 665.

Bovet, D., Bovet-Nitti, F., Oliverio, A. (Eds.) (1968) *Recent Advances in Learning and Retention*. Rome: Accademia Nazionale dei Lincei.

Church, R. M. (1969) 'Response suppression.' *in* Campbell, B. A., Church, R. M. (Eds.) *Punishment and Aversive Behavior*. New York: Appleton-Century-Crofts.

Connolly, K. (1969) 'Sensory-motor co-ordination.' *in* Wolff, P. H., Mac Keith, R. (Eds.) *Planning for Better Learning*. Clinics in Developmental Medicine, No. 33. London: S.I.M.P. with Heinemann. p. 20.

Crook, J. H. (1971) 'Sources of cooperation in animals and man.' *in* Eisenberg, J. F., Dillon, W. S. (Eds.) *Man and Beast: Comparative Social Behavior*. Washington: Smithsonian Institution.

Denenberg, V. H., Whimbey, A. E. (1963) 'Behavior of adult rats is modified by the experiences their mothers had as infants.' *Science*, **142**, 1192.

Eibl-Eibesfeldt, I., Hass, H. (1967) 'Neue Wege der Humanethologie.' *Homo*, **18**, 13.

Eisenberg, J. F., Dillon, W. S. (Eds.) (1971) *Man and Beast: Comparative Social Behavior*. Washington: Smithsonian Institution.

Ekman, P., Friesen, W. V. (1969) 'The repertoire of nonverbal behavior: categories, origins, usage, and coding.' *Semiotica*, **1**, 49.

Ford, E. B. (1964) *Ecological Genetics*. London: Methuen.

Forgus, R. H. (1955) 'Early visual and motor experience as determiners of complex maze-learning ability.' *Journal of Comparative and Physiological Psychology*, **48**, 215.

Fowler, H., Wischner, G. J. (1969) 'The varied functions of punishment in discrimination learning.' *in* Campbell, B. A., Church, R. M. (Eds.) *Punishment and Aversive Behavior*. New York: Appleton-Century-Crofts.

Freeman, R. D., Mitchell, D. E., Millodot, M. (1972) 'A neural effect of partial visual deprivation in humans.' *Science*, **175**, 1384.

Gibson, E. J., Walk, R. D. (1956) 'The effect of prolonged exposure to visually presented patterns on learning to discriminate them.' *Journal of Comparative and Physiological Psychology*, **49**, 239.

Hallowell, A. I. (1960) 'Self, society and culture in phylogenetic perspective.' in Tax, S. (Ed.) *Evolution After Darwin. Vol. 2. The Evolution of Man*. Chicago: University of Chicago Press. p. 309.

Harlow, H. F. (1959) 'The development of learning in the rhesus monkey.' *American Scientist*, **47**, 459.

Hebb, D. O. (1949) *The Organization of Behavior*. New York: Wiley.

Held, R., Bauer, J. A. (1967) 'Visually guided reaching in infant monkeys after restricted rearing.' *Science*, **155**, 718.

—— Hein, A. (1963) 'Movement-produced stimulation in the development of visually guided behavior.' *Journal of Comparative and Physiological Psychology*, **56**, 872.

Hinde, R. A., Spencer-Booth, Y. (1971) 'Effects of brief separation from mother on rhesus monkeys.' *Science*, **173**, 111.

Hogben, L. (1933) *Nature and Nurture*. London: Allen & Unwin.

Jensen, G. D., Bobbitt, R. A., Gordon, B. N. (1968) 'Effects of environment on the relationship between mother and infant pigtailed monkeys (*Macaca nemestrina*).' *Journal of Comparative and Physiological Psychology*, **66**, 259.

Kagan, J. (1971) *Change and Continuity in Infancy*. New York: Wiley.

Lancaster, J. B. (1971) 'Play-mothering: the relations between juvenile females and young infants among free-ranging vervet monkeys (*Cercopithecus aethiops*).' *Folia Primatologica*, **15**, 161.

Loizos, C. (1966) 'Play in mammals.' *Symposia of the Zoological Society of London*, **18**, 1.

Lovejoy, A. O. (1960) *The Great Chain of Being*. New York: Harper.

Mackintosh, N. J. (1969) 'Comparative studies of reversal and probability learning: rats, birds and fish.' *in* Gilbert, R. M., Sutherland, N. S. (Eds.) *Animal Discrimination Learning*. London: Academic Press.

Marx, M. H. (1944) 'The effects of cumulative training upon retroactive inhibition and transfer.' *Comparative Psychology Monographs*, **18**, (2). (Serial no. 94.)

Mead, M. (1971) 'Innate behavior and building new cultures: a commentary.' *in* Eisenberg, J. F., Dillon, W. S. (Eds.) *Man and Beast: Comparative Social Behavior*. Washington: Smithsonian Institution.

Razran, G. (1971) *Mind in Evolution*. Boston: Houghton Mifflin.

Ressler, R. H. (1963) 'Genotype-correlated parental influences in two strains of mice.' *Journal of Comparative and Physiological Psychology*, **56**, 882.

—— (1966) 'Inherited environmental influences on the operant behavior of mice.' *Journal of Comparative and Physiological Psychology*, **61**, 264.

Shlaer, R. (1971) 'Shift in binocular disparity causes compensatory change in the cortical structure of kittens.' *Science*, **173**, 638.

Singer, C. (1917) 'A review of the medical literature of the dark ages, with a new text of about 1110.' *Proceedings of the Royal Society of Medicine, Section of the History of Medicine*, **10**, 110.

Tobach, E. Schneirla, T. C. (1962) 'Eliminative responses in mice and rats and the problem of "emotionality".' in Bliss, E. L. (Ed.) *Roots of Behavior*. New York: Hoeber.

White, B. L., Castle, P., Held, R. (1964) 'Observations on the development of visually-directed reaching.' *Child Development*, **35**, 349.

Wolff, P. H., Mac Keith, R. (Eds.) (1969) *Planning for Better Learning*. Clinics in Developmental Medicine, No. 33. London: S.I.M.P. with Heinemann.

Author Index